Beyond Solitude

A Cache of Alaska Tales

Jo Massey

Copyright 2004

ISBN# 1-932636-09-9   softcover

Library of Congress Control Number: 2004108219

A version of *Two Thumbs Up* has appeared in *Visual Eyes, Verbalize*,
a literary publication of Northwest College, Powell, Wyoming.

Versions of *Dolly's Revenge* and *An Act of Nature*
have both been winners in Wyoming Writer's Inc. writing contests,
and were published in that organization's anthologies.

Cover Design: Antelope Design
Cover Art: Seth Dotson
Published by Pronghorn Press

www.pronghornpress.org

*Dedicated, in memoriam
to my husband, Bruce A. Massey
—a truly great storyteller.*

Acknowledgments

Thanks to my four delightful daughters, who each in their own way added to the quality of this collection with their encouragement, comments, and approval: Tamela Bury, Roxan Jones, Heidi Pamplin, and—with a special note of thanks—Heather Breckenridge-Dawson. Many of the storylines are stronger because of her astute observations and candid feedback.

My wonderful editor and friend, Claude Dotson, deserves special mention. His keen editorial comments and unfailing belief in my work, his words of encouragement and gentle nudges have all been instrumental in the project's completion.

I appreciate the nurturing and constructive critiques of many fellow writers and friends, including the members of Cody Writer's Group, Wyoming Writers, Inc., and Cheyenne Area Writers Group.

With gratitude and love to my trusted friend and companion, Ken Johnston. His generosity in sharing his first hand experiences as biologist on Saint Paul Island and as a Denali park ranger, helped ensure accuracy in descriptions of Alaska backcountry. He also patiently suffered through the process of reading many revisions and drafts, often finding errors others missed.

Finally, kudos go to my exceptional editor and publisher, Annette Chaudet. Her abilities as writer and artist always amaze me, and I am proud to call her friend. Thanks for hours of great conversation and for making this book a reality.

With deep gratitude in memoriam to the artist, Seth Dotson, BFA University of Idaho, for the cover design. It is from his original painting, Watchful Wolf, one of his last works. At the age of twenty-two, he died tragically in a car crash May 31, 2002, and only a few expressions of his beautiful vision remain.

Contents

The fictional characters that people this book have each experienced a very personal form of solitude as they confront the challenges of isolation, both physical and emotional. And while the stories deal with the basic human need for connection, there is also humor here as many of them find unique ways to adapt.

Fresh Start

Jo Massey

Sylvia knew she was teetering on the edge of insanity. It had been five months, yet the scene replayed in her mind as clearly as if it had been only this morning. Strange how she seemed to remember it more clearly now than she had at the time, lying there on the delivery room table, her legs still in the stirrups, bare bottom exposed to the world.

"Push, Mrs. Bradshaw," the doctor had said. She'd pushed.

Then, even though she'd sensed accelerated activity around her, the sounds in the room had suddenly ceased after that final thrust of energy. She wished they would cover her up—she was freezing. Questions laboriously formed in her drugged mind. Is it a boy or girl? Why don't I hear crying? Where did everyone go? How long has it been? She dozed, her senses fading in and out like a late-night AM radio station.

When the doctor woke her, her legs were still spread, and even though a thin, white sheet covered them, she shivered violently. The room seemed even colder now that the strong overhead lamps had been turned out.

"I'm so terribly sorry, Sylvia. We did all we could but the child was stillborn." She couldn't seem to comprehend what the doctor said, instead pushing the words from her mind as she slipped back to sleep.

She could feel herself being washed, pads being put into place, her legs lowered onto the delivery table, a blanket placed over them. Was this an hallucination, a bad dream brought on by the drugs? What did he mean?

She tried to drag herself back to the room. "Where's my baby?" she asked, looking for the doctor who had already left. Only a poker-faced nurse was left, bustling about, tidying up.

Suddenly more alert and awake she insisted again, "Where's my baby?"

"Your baby's dead," came the insensitive reply.

Things at home had only gotten worse after that. Johnny, her husband of two years, quit his job. Said he couldn't stand putting bolts into little holes, eight hours a day, day in and day out. Said he wasn't 'raised to work in no factory like some wetback.' Said he'd get another job—a better paying job—any time he wanted. Only he hadn't been able to find any job, never mind one that paid more. So they couldn't pay the rent for the cute little house on the quiet street behind the library. They'd had to move out.

Johnny's dad let them have one of his tacky little rental apartments in exchange for Johnny's help with yard maintenance. Her mom, who had extensive first-hand knowledge of the nuances of the state's welfare system, had coached Sylvia in applying for all the social services available.

They had a roof and food, but that was all. She was deeply unhappy and depressed.

It was nearly noon Saturday morning and she had not yet dressed. She sat in the middle of their rumpled bed, her knees drawn into her chest, mournfully staring at peeling red polish on her stubby toes. Her bare thighs, unaccustomed to the extra weight she'd put on in recent months, felt tight, the skin stretched thin and taut. Her normal pink complexion, now sallow and splotchy, accentuated the dark circles that rimmed her expressionless blue eyes. Blond hair, badly in need of washing and brushing, lay limp and lusterless across her forehead and neck.

Despite sunshine outside, a depressive gray aura that seemed to emanate from her filled the studio apartment.

"I hate this stinkin' hole," she suddenly screamed, throwing her pillow across the room. She partially blamed the cramped little apartment for the changes in Johnny.

He spent as much time away as possible, always with his friends—most of it down at the bar drinking, shooting pool, watching football games on the TV—or else he was out joyriding around the countryside with his buddies, or who-knows-what-else.

When the door to the little apartment opened a short time later, Sylvia had curled back into the bed and lay staring at the ceiling, much in need of paint. Johnny bounced into the bedroom, leaped onto the bed with his boots still on and began jumping up and down on it like a little kid whose parents weren't watching. Sylvia tried to ignore his bizarre behavior, but it was impossible to stay steady in the jiggling bed.

She sat up. "What's the matter with you, John William

Bradshaw?" she asked, using his full name as if she were his cross mother.

"Get up and start packing," he said. "We're going on an adventure. Come on, Sparkie, get a move on." She couldn't remember the last time he'd used the pet name he'd given her when they first began dating. "We're leaving Boise and going to Alaska," he said. "I got a job with Martin's uncle."

Sylvia didn't like his friend, Martin. She blamed him for so often keeping Johnny out late at night.

"He's got a fishing boat and needs another hand. It's only for the summer, but it pays big bucks. Probably won't get rich, but it'll sure set us up for better times."

Something in the gaiety of his mood was infectious and in spite of her depression she felt a glimmer of excitement. She rolled over and looked into his face, seeing a childlike exuberance. He stopped jumping on the bed and dropped to his knees next to her. He bent over and kissed her, long and hard on the mouth, something he'd not done in months. At first she was reluctant, then responded hungrily to the pressure of his lips on her own. The release of sex was rushed, concluded in a flurry, leaving them both spent but it somehow seemed to glue together some of the broken shards of their floundering marriage.

One week later, with everything of value that they owned stuffed into the ten-year-old Ford sedan Johnny's father had give them as a going-away gift, they started out. They made the trip in six days, stopping at night in whatever pullout or camping spot they could find. By the end of the second night, her face was puffy and swollen from all the mosquito bites she'd suffered sleeping in the open, their sleeping bags tossed out on the ground because he was too tired to put up the tent.

Sylvia begged him to stop here and there so she could snap a picture with her cheap camera, and occasionally he indulged her—their first moose sighting, for instance, and totem poles in Whitehorse, and once, a wolf loping into the timber just off the edge of the highway. He stopped so she could take his picture as he pretended to study the markings on the "Mile Post Zero" cairn in the center of Dawson Creek and again along an empty stretch of road near Kluane Lake when he was in the midst of changing their second flat, his shirt sleeves rolled to the shoulder showing hard muscles. Any other photos she wanted she had to be content to take only when they stopped for lunch or to relieve themselves.

True to his word, Martin's uncle, Jim Muldoon, was ready for Johnny to start work almost immediately when they'd arrived. They set up their tent in Sweeney's Campground just outside town, and it wasn't so bad with the tent to help protect them from the mosquitoes. Housing was hard to find and they hadn't had any luck finding a place before Johnny put out to sea with the fishing fleet. He gave Sylvia what little money they had left, instructing her to find a place and 'dicker on the rent.' "We've got to live cheap," he warned. "We're going to save every penny of what I earn, if we can."

She spent the next several days unsuccessfully combing the town for someplace where they could afford to live. By late in the afternoon on the fifth day she was so discouraged that even a room with a shared bath would have looked good. Homesick and worried about the steadily depleting money in her purse, she wandered into Betty's Cafe to get a sandwich.

As it was between the lunch and dinner crowds, Betty was alone in the cafe. "Hello, honey," she said in a motherly tone. "You must be the wife of Jim's new hand. I heard there was a new young couple in town."

"Yes," Sylvia said, surprised that this pleasant, stout woman would know of her. "We just got here five days ago. My husband is out on the boat now."

"Oh, yes, all the able-bodied men are out. The town seems pretty quiet without the bunch of them here causing trouble," Betty chuckled. "I'm joking; they're a good bunch of old boys, really. It'd be a pretty lonely place around here without the men folk." Sylvia wondered if she would miss Johnny all that much if he weren't around.

"I've been trying to find a place to live but haven't had any luck yet," she said after giving Betty her order for a plain toasted cheese sandwich and a glass of milk.

"I heard you've been camped out at Sweeney's Campground," Betty said. "I started out there myself, many years ago, when Charlie and I first moved here. I know how quickly that can become tiresome. Charlie was my husband. We'd been married forty-three years when he died a couple of years back."

"I'm so sorry," Sylvia said. She couldn't think of anything else to say, so she began eating the sandwich Betty placed before her. She was hungrier than she'd realized and for a few moments she just ate, chewing thoughtfully. She realized Betty was watching her discreetly from the end of the counter. She swallowed a drink of milk and then asked,

"I don't suppose you know of any place, do you?"

Betty looked at her thoughtfully. "Well," she said slowly, "I do have a spare room in my living quarters in back. It isn't much, but it's in out of the cold and bugs. I guess I could let you stay here for a while, until you find something else, that is. I'm afraid it wouldn't do for a couple, though, but since your husband will be gone more than he's here, it might work out for the time being."

Sylvia stared at her, wondering at first if she was really serious about her offer. The kindly look on Betty's face assured her.

"Oh, wow," she said. "That would really be great. Maybe I could help you out here in the restaurant, too. I do have some experience waiting tables."

"Perfect," Betty said. "It's a done deal, then. I could use some more help around here. When you finish eating, run back out to the campground and bring your things in. I'll make up the bed with clean sheets and have it ready for you."

The arrangement suited both women well. Sylvia thrived under the motherly care of Betty and loved working in the cheery atmosphere of the cafe. That Betty enjoyed having her around was obvious to even the most casual observer. They were a team, each anticipating the actions of the other, and the business—already a well-established part of the community—seemed to increase, becoming the hub where folks gathered to eat or to just pass the time and gossip. Slowly, the painful memory of the loss of her baby and the associated depression began to fade as she made friends.

Mid-season, when the fleet was in town on their break, Johnny came into the cafe during the noon rush hour.

"I'm leaving this stinking little town and going back to Idaho after fishing is over," he announced loudly enough for everyone to hear. Then, turning to Betty who was refilling coffee mugs around the cafe, he said, "You'd better start looking for another waitress. My wife will be leaving."

Sylvia stared at him, stunned. "I'm not leaving," she said. The words spilled out of her mouth before she could think. She was aware that the entire noon crowd had turned toward them. "I'm not leaving," she repeated, this time with full conviction.

Johnny acted like she'd slapped him. Then after a moment he shrugged. "Suit yourself," he said angrily and slammed out the door.

For a few moments the cafe was totally quiet, all the customers now busily eating, pretending they'd not been witness to this exchange. But Sylvia couldn't help noticing the sympathetic looks as she carried heaping platters of food to their tables and took empty ones back to the kitchen.

Only one person mentioned anything about the scene to her. As he paid his check, Mark O'Brien leaned his tall lanky body across the cash register towards her and whispered, "He's a jerk. Sorry, Sylvia, but that's the way I see it."

She didn't respond, only watched him get in his pickup and turn back towards his office at the airport. She remembered those words later when she heard the engines of his small plane fly overhead.

After that Johnny stayed in the tent at the campground any time he was in town. He only dropped by the cafe to eat and pretend he was there to see his wife. She knew he spent most of his free time with his friends at Shorty's bar, and his visits to the restaurant were short and without any warmth or affection.

A couple of weeks later when Johnny came into the cafe, a woman was with him. She dragged a small boy behind her and Sylvia observed that the child walked with a noticeable limp. The threesome sat at a corner table and when she approached to take their food order, Johnny looked up at her with defiance on his face. "This is Carrie," he said. "I have to take her to Anchorage on business, and she needs someone to take care of the kid while we're gone. I told her you'd do it."

Sylvia blanched at his boldness, too shocked to speak. "Do you want to order something to eat?" was all she could muster in response.

Carrie looked uncertainly at Johnny, who sat studying the menu, even though he knew it by heart. "Bring her a hamburger with fries. And I'll have the T-bone, rare. You know how I like it."

"What about the little boy?" Sylvia asked.

"Oh, just a hot dog will be fine." She looked at the mother to see if that was what she wanted for the child, but Carrie was engrossed in Johnny, who seemed to be ignoring them all.

Then Sylvia noticed the little boy smiling at her, his blue eyes unusually large, the black pupils clear and innocent. She smiled back and asked him. "Do you want some French fries, too?" He vigorously nodded, his blond curls bobbing with the action.

Her hands shook as she handed the meal order to

Betty, busy in the kitchen. "I heard that," Betty said with disgust. "You aren't going to let him get away with that, are you?"

"I don't know what to do," she replied, picking up Mark O'Brien's order and carrying it to him where he sat at the counter. His shock of red hair seemed more unruly than normal, and she tried to avoid his eyes, knowing he, too, had witnessed the strange episode. He cleared his throat as if to speak, but when he did it was only to say, "Will you bring me some catsup?" She was aware that his eyes followed her as she got it for him.

Sylvia went into the kitchen where she could observe the dining room without being noticed. She watched the three people sitting at the corner table. Johnny and Carrie were holding hands, staring into each other's eyes—obviously lovers—ignoring the child sitting quietly and alone beside them. She was not surprised, nor did she feel any particular anguish. But as she looked at the boy, so sweet and innocent, her heart melted. Then she noticed the brace on his leg and understood the limp.

When their food order was up, she delivered the meal as if these were just regular customers, in normal conditions. "Can I bring you anything else?" she asked, her voice polite.

"No. This is just fine," Johnny said, his mouth already filled with steak. "Well, what about it? Will you watch the kid?"

Sylvia held her voice steady. "When are you going and how long will you be gone? I have to work, you know. He'd have to stay here in the cafe with me."

"Oh, he won't be a problem." His mother spoke now

for the first time. "He's very good. I have some clean clothes for him in the car."

"We're leaving right after we eat," Johnny informed her. "We'll probably be back in four days. I have to go back to work on Friday."

The child looked from one adult to another as this exchange went on, finally focusing fully on Sylvia. "What is your name?" she asked him.

"Timmy," he said proudly.

"Hi, Timmy. My name is Sylvia," she said. He gave her a big smile. "How old are you, Timmy?"

With one hand he worked to hold down the thumb and little finger of the opposite hand. "I'm free," he said. She smiled back at him.

When Johnny came back to the register to pay the bill she said, "Ok, I'll watch him," she said to Johnny.

"Thanks," he said. "You're a good sport, Syl. We'll be back Thursday, unless something happens." Only then did she allow herself to drop the polite facade. Her look should have told him that, at that moment, she wished him dead. He was already on his way out the door and didn't see it. But Mark did.

Timmy's mother had been correct when she said he would not be a problem. Betty and Sylvia kept him occupied while they worked. He spent hours happily playing in the kitchen, clanging spoons on pots and pans, or carving out cookie dough with a variety of clever animal shaped cutters, or driving a collection of cars—donated by some of the customers—around the edges of the room, then parking them in a cabinet that served as a garage, cleaned out for just that purpose. He was content sitting at the counter with a coloring book and crayons, usually chatting brightly with the customers. He had quickly wormed his way into the hearts of not only Sylvia and Betty, but the community as well.

In the evening, either Sylvia or Betty read him stories after he'd had a bath and his brace was reattached to the crooked little limb. Then, sleepy and satisfied, he was tucked into one side of Sylvia's bed. Later, when she crawled in beside him, she would brush a blond curl from his forehead and kiss him.

Two weeks passed. No one had heard from Johnny or Timmy's mother. And Sylvia had begun to worry. Then, even though she hated to admit it, she realized that she'd allowed a small glimmer of hope into her mind.

Sylvia was behind the counter making a fresh pot of coffee when an official looking black car pulled up outside the cafe and a man and woman, both dressed in suits, entered. When Betty directed them to a clean table, the man flashed a badge and said, "We're with the Alaska Department of Human Services. I understand you have a child here by the name of Timothy Mickelson. We're here to take him."

Sylvia's heart skipped a beat, her hands turned clammy, and she felt her face suddenly flush, the rush of anxiety nearly incapacitating her for a moment. She stood rigid, rooted to the spot, as time seemed to cease.

Finally she heard Betty's voice, likewise concerned. "I don't understand. Where's his mother?" she asked.

"Miss Mickelson has signed papers giving ward of the child to the State. It's right here," the female social worker stated. "He will be placed in a foster home as soon as one can be found."

Suddenly Sylvia was propelled by an energy that didn't seem to come from her and she ran to where Betty and the two State employees stood. "Please, let him stay here with us. We'll take care of him. He's very happy here and we love him," she blurted out, not once thinking about consulting her employer.

"She's right," Betty said in full agreement. "Tell us what we must do in order to satisfy the State's requirements."

"I'm sorry. We've been sent to collect the child," the man said. "We can't leave him, not without the proper authorization. And there's the matter of the medical care he needs, an operation to straighten his leg."

Before he finished his argument, Betty had them all seated at a table and she had begun creating a convincing case, filled with reasons why and ways that would allow Timmy to stay with them.

In the end, after a number of telephone consultations, and a stack of paperwork, the two social workers left without taking the little blue-eyed boy with them. "It will all take time," they said, "and you must understand that he could be removed at any time if or when another more suitable home becomes available."

Things went well with each subsequent visit from the welfare office. They were still looking for a more traditional foster home for Timmy until adoptive parents could be found, but in the meantime, they finally seemed to be convinced that he could not receive any better care than he was getting. And it seemed to Betty and Sylvia that they weren't trying too hard to find somewhere else to place him. Sylvia never allowed herself to think of the day when adoptive parents would appear and take him from her. She knew first hand the pain of losing a child and she knew losing Timmy would be more than she could bear.

Just before Christmas, when the path leading into Betty's Cafe was snow-packed and festive red and green lights twinkled among the icicles hanging from the eaves, Sylvia received a short note from Johnny, the first since he'd left. He had gone back home as he said he would, taking Carrie with him, but she'd soon tired of him and moved out, leaving him for someone else. He apologized for his behavior and asked her to come home. He was broke, of course, so couldn't send her money to come, but suggested she borrow enough from Betty to make the trip. "We can start over," he wrote. "We both made mistakes, but I'm willing to give you another chance."

When she finished the letter, she handed it to Mark. He was sitting in his usual spot at the counter, watching her as she read. "He's a jerk," she said, repeating the same words he'd used before to describe Johnny. "You were absolutely right."

"What are you going to do?" he asked after he'd finished reading the letter. There was concern in his voice.

"File for a divorce, now that I know where he is," she laughed. "What would you expect me to do?" She couldn't help but notice the light in his eyes as he smiled.

He took a drink from his mug, holding it against his lower lip even after he'd swallowed, as if thinking. "Hey, I have an idea," he finally said. "Tomorrow, on your day off, how would you and Timmy like to go for a ride in the plane?"

She didn't even have to think about it. "That would really be super," she said, smiling. When Timmy's excitement made it so hard for him to fall asleep that night, she almost wished she'd kept the trip a secret until it was time to go.

They arrived at the airport early the next morning. Timmy wriggled excitedly as Mark strapped him into a seat in the back. Sylvia, too, felt animated. This was her first flight in a small plane. She watched Mark as he spun the propeller, thinking how young he looked, even though she knew he was twenty-eight. He had that kind of face.

Even with the short daylight hours, it could not have been more perfect—the sun skimming above the southern horizon in a clear blue sky, temperatures cold and exhilarating.

They flew in a wide circle over the town as Mark pointed out familiar landmarks below. Then he took them out over the waters of the inlet where they looked for black and white killer whales. The fact that they didn't see any didn't diminish their fun. Then they headed towards mountains—majestic purple peaks, snowcapped and regal— towering in the distance.

Directly below were miles of marshy tundra, lumpy and frozen under the snow and broken only by stands of willow. Timmy, his little face pressed to the window, sat totally engrossed in all the sights passing below. Suddenly, he pointed and shouted, "Look, Mommy! A moose!"

His words—that name—filled her with joy. Unbidden, a tear sprang into her eye and as she looked at Mark, he reached across the space between them, smiled and squeezed her hand.

When they were back on the ground, Timmy sighed a deep sigh. "I want to be a pilot when I grow up," he said wistfully.

"Me too," Sylvia said. "Maybe we'll all be pilots some day."

Grisly Alibi

Jo Massey

How had this happened—this grisly thing—this awful event that, even in your most horrifying nightmares, you'd never dream could happen to you? It's one of those things you think might only happen to other people, very few other people at that. And those who have something like this catch them by surprise, are people who live on the edge, tempting fate with irresponsible behavior, prone to foolhardy bravado— the risk takers. Things like this don't happen to bank tellers, with run-of-the-mill husbands, and two boringly-normal children, both of average intelligence—an ordinary, all-American family seeking only some degree of normalcy and whatever creature comforts their combined incomes would tolerate.

In the two weeks since it happened, I've recounted the story over and over again, until it sounds, even to me who lived through it, unbelievable, absurd, bizarre, ridiculous, all the adjectives expressed by the authorities—the local sheriff, Fish and Game wardens, the news people, our minister, and yes, even my own father, who was—or so I thought—as fair-minded as any man on earth could be!

They've all accused me of lying; they've alluded that at best I'm hysterical, even worse, delusional—or most horribly, I'm a cold-blooded murderer, conjuring this story to cover up my guilt!

Oh, they seem convinced of my guilt. At first I was only questioned. But since then I've been arrested, fingerprinted, photographed, allowed my one-only phone call, spent three nights in jail waiting a bail hearing, posted bond, and been questioned again and again by all the people who have some interest in the matter.

Now I sit at home, waiting my day in court, with the curtains drawn, too embarrassed to answer the door, or the telephone, or to show up at work. Oh, I see them—those people walking by our house, staring, pointing, apparently with hopes of getting a peek at the "husband killer." People are all too much like predators, quick to pounce on and devour anyone who appears weak or vulnerable. I feel like a piece of bait, sitting here in my solitude, rotting away a little more each day, just waiting for the moment when I'll be torn to shreds, eaten sinew by sinew, bone by bone, my blood spilled before the world, as it watches in hyena-like pleasure. I seem to hear them laughing even now.

I should have known the trip would end in disaster. All the warning signs were there, if only I'd paid attention to my intuition. If only I hadn't let him persuade me. He could be very persuasive with "that" look—one corner of his lip raised in a sneer, his squinting eyes made expressive by that thing he did with his eyebrows—the left one lifted in an arch, the right creased and pulled down over the eyeball like a black cape. The entire look need last only a fraction of a second, yet all of its meaning was there, bare naked, not to be misunderstood nor defied.

"Ok, I'll go if I must," I said, putting my own plans for the weekend out of my mind, knowing that if I refused his demand I'd surely pay later. "But why can't Bill or Jake go with you?" I knew my voice sounded whiney, but I couldn't suppress my irritation.

"You think I wouldn't rather have one of them? It ain't 'cause I especially want you to go, you know. It's only that it isn't safe for a guy to go out alone, that's all," he said. "Anyhow, I've asked both of them, plus everyone else I could think of, but they all have other stuff to do—mostly stuff to keep their women happy." A chauvinistic look of disgust flitted across his face.

So, come Saturday morning, we left the kids with my friends, Francine and Jim Muldoon, who are like grandparents to them, and we set off on the ill-fated journey to a remote lake in search of the biggest bull moose he could find.

The first dark omen came as we were unloading our gear from the Super Cub. We'd formed a relay—Clint, our pilot, stood on one of the floats handing things to my husband, Cal. Cal, in turn, passed them on to me, and I stacked everything a little further up the beach. We were nearly finished when, even though my arms were filled, Cal added his new Ruger and holster to the top of my load. When I turned to set the load down, the pistol slid out of the holster, and clattered to the ground, hitting hard and bouncing off a boulder.

"Goddamnit, woman," he shouted, striking me hard across the cheek with the back of his hand. "Look what you've done!"

He picked the weapon up and caressed it gently, rubbing his fingers across the steel barrel, turning it over and over until he was able to detect a small ding on the polished wooden grip.

He glared at me. "My goddamn new pistol—wrecked!" He stalked away carrying his precious gun like it was an injured child.

I caught Clint staring at me and then he turned, obviously embarrassed at what he'd just witnessed. I could feel an angry flush rising on my cheek from where he'd struck me, matching the humiliation of this ugly scene. My mood was just as angry. "Sometimes he makes me so frigging mad, I could just kill him," I cursed.

Clint slowly turned back towards me, with a quick look of shock. "Just a figure of speech," I said. I shrugged and attempted a smile.

A cloud of mosquitoes swarmed around my head as I reluctantly watched Clint climb back into the cockpit and start the engine. Annoyed, I swatted at the pesky insects. A feeling of anxiety washed over me as I saw the Super Cub move away across the water, bouncing over its own waves, gaining momentum. A few moments later it lifted into the air, banked sharply, circled overhead, then headed back towards Anchorage, roughly two hundred and fifty miles away. He would return for us in four days, but until then it was just the two of us out here, alone, against the wilderness.

The plane shrank, becoming smaller and smaller until

it appeared to be no more than a toy. It was finally gobbled up by the milky-blue autumn sky. Again I was aware of that knot of uneasiness squeezing my chest. Somehow, standing here in the middle of nowhere with no way of leaving, four days seemed like an eternity.

When at last I turned from the now empty sky, I saw Cal had already dragged most of our gear further up the beach and was clearing a spot to pitch our tent next to a thicket of bushes. He whistled as he kicked stones and branches off the place he'd chosen. I always marveled at how he could get mad so quickly and just as rapidly get over it. I'm different. It takes a lot, usually, for me to get mad, but once I do it takes a long time to burn out.

He stopped suddenly and bent close to study the ground. A long, slow whistle escaped from his lips. "Would you look at this," he said, motioning me over. "Biggest damn moose tracks I think I've ever seen!"

I looked, obligingly, trying to muster up some emotion of excitement, but still unable to shake off my anger and feeling of foreboding. "Umm," I murmured. I just couldn't work myself into a hunter's frenzy over killing animals, even for food.

As I helped prepare our camp, I tried to analyze my dark feelings, searching for some way to dispel my sense of dread. I wondered if it came entirely from my reluctance—my initial resentment at feeling forced to come—or was it the recent ugly incident? I didn't think so, because I'd had this uneasiness from the start. The cloud of biting mosquitoes did nothing to help my mood, especially when I realized they were not bothering Cal.

I tried sternly to reassure myself. Cal was a very experienced outdoorsman and hunter; he'd spent hours preparing for all contingencies that could arise on this trip. The weather was expected to stay clear, but alternative plans had been made in the event of unforeseen bad weather; we had ample food supplies for extra days, and we were both in good physical condition. Some hard work to get ready, but the rewards of solitude and quiet to be found in this remote country—away from both of our demanding jobs, the kids, his parents, and our various extracurricular activities we seem to overindulge in—more than offset the labor involved preparing for the trip.

I slapped at another mosquito, shrugged, and shook my head as if to shake off my negativity. Itchy red welts began to appear where I'd been bitten. In spite of that, I decided to try to make the best of things and attempt to enjoy the outing. Maybe this time alone together would help us get our marriage back on track. Lord knows it could use some help, and I, for one, was willing to make the effort for the kids' sake, if not for any other reason. Maybe this would prove to be a special event for us—probably what we've needed for a long time. I nearly convinced myself that everything would work out fine.

I walked back down the beach to search for the can of insect repellent and gather the rest of our gear. I lavishly sprayed myself, not caring if I now reeked of insecticide. Once I felt adequately protected from being eaten alive, I looked more closely at the scenery surrounding us. The lake lay east and, by Alaska standards, was small—a quarter mile of shoreline here at the narrow end before it fanned out broadly a short distance further on, covering about two square miles, mostly surrounded by alder, with the one exception of the sandy beach where we landed. A jetty of rock extended out into the water from the right side for six or eight feet, a narrow finger of solid ground where animals could walk out to drink; however, I supposed most animals would come to the beach since I'd observed a multitude of animal tracks up and down the strip of sand.

A hundred and eighty degrees opposite, to the west, was a broad river valley that fed the lake. This late in the year it was reduced to a series of shallow channels, intertwining occasionally, forming what looked like, from the air, a loose braid of sand, laced with murky glacial-gray ribbons of water. Scattered across the river valley, as if to add green sprigs of color, thickets of brush randomly dotted the sand dunes.

On either side of the valley, hills rose gradually up; the southern one was covered with heavy growth of alder extending to the water's edge. The northern slope, due to its southern exposure was more open, with thick low-lying underbrush along the riverbank—some of it probably muskeg—before it climbed to occasional stands of alder higher up the bank.

I slung my backpack over a shoulder, grabbed the box containing our cooking gear, and carried them back to our campsite. Cal had the tent staked down and stood glassing the valley with his spotting scope.

"You think there's a bull here that's bigger than Jake's record one?" I asked.

"Damned straight there is," he said. "Clint said he's seen bunches of 'em up the river every time he flies over here.

There's one really big old boy that he's spotted more'n once—one a damn site bigger'n that flea-bitten one Jake's so proud of. This bull must be an old bugger. He's a loner—likes to hide out in the dense trees. He's been seen in this very watershed recently."

I found myself involuntarily scanning the tree line to the north, watching for any kind of movement. A big bull moose can do a lot of damage if he doesn't fancy you being in his territory.

"Well, I hope you have your chance at him," I said, halfheartedly, scratching the red welts on my hands and neck. All I could think about was all the work involved in packing out one of those huge animals. The head alone, with a big rack of horns attached, ideal for mounting and "gracing" our wall, would be all the two of us could manage together. Of course, Cal always said the main reason to kill was for food, and to be sure, we could use the meat. It would be good to have both deep freezers filled, which could be done with one good-sized moose. But I'd never be convinced that a rack of impressive antlers wasn't his real goal.

"Hey, let's go out and have a look around," Cal said suddenly.

We started out toward the southern bank, stepping across a couple of rivulets in the first half-mile, before entering the trees. There were moose signs aplenty in the loose sand along the way. Piles of droppings—some, but not all, very fresh—the size, shape and color of over-ripe wild plums, strangely reminded me of the dark hairy mole on Cal's back. Footprints shaped somewhat like their cousin, the deer—but not nearly as delicate—crisscrossed each other on numerous routes to the water's edge. The difference somehow reminded me of the Cinderella story, the part where her ungainly stepsisters' big feet kept them from slipping on the dainty glass slipper, proving they weren't the princess-to-be.

As we entered the trees I shuddered. I literally felt oppressive dark shadows; the heavy thicket of alders grasped at my clothes, like grotesque, boney fingers of giant corpses, intent on stopping me from pushing deeper into the dreary gloom. Scaly bark snatched at my hair, the branches scratched my hands and arms, forcing me to stop to untangle myself from them. I'd forgotten the aggravating way these Sitka alders have of growing branches from nearly ground level, all the way up their trunks, and at odd intervals, making passage through them nearly impossible at times—especially if you have a pack on your back. It's like trying to bend low enough to clear a limbo stick and jump rope at the same time. Try that with a pack!

The sounds of Cal's footsteps became fainter and fainter as he pushed ahead, leaving me in his wake, struggling to free myself. I thought once to call out to him, to beg him to stop and wait, but decided it would be useless anyway. He was on a mission and wouldn't be happy if he were detained.

I battled deeper into the dim, trying to follow the path he had forced. But, of course, there was no real "path," only occasional telltale signs where branches appeared freshly bent or where the soil had been scuffed. Clouds of mosquitoes rose from the underbrush—still annoying—but, thankfully, they only swarmed around my eyes and nose, and didn't bite.

Suddenly, I heard an eerie sound, like the mournful wail of someone or something in pain. I froze. It seemed to be coming from further up the hill, a short distance ahead. I held my breath and listened. There it was again—a sound like none I've every heard—then a long pause. I strained my ears to hear, and when it came again I eased forward, creeping as quietly as I could, climbing the slope, wishing Cal were somewhere near. Sometimes, even poor companionship is better than being alone, I thought.

Now the sound came from just ahead. I sucked in a shallow breath and shakily moved still closer. Then, with a gasp of relief I saw a dead tree leaning into another; they were sawing against each other in the afternoon wind. Still, their lamentation seemed to be a portent of things to come.

My nerves were so taut, and the subsequent relief so profound, I suddenly felt the need to empty my bladder. I squatted right where I was, and wished I could empty my long pent-up emotions as easily. I felt like I could "cry a river." Cry for the lonely, loveless nights, sharing the same set of sheets with my husband, yet always facing his back—a wall that'd become almost impossible to climb over. Cry for years of exile from my own family, for all the tiny disappointments now stacked high and which—like the mountain, McKinley— are seldom seen, so often hidden under clouds of forgetfulness.

My reverie exploded when a rifle shot reverberated through the air, somewhere ahead of me. I bolted up, grabbing at my jeans, jerking them to cover my naked behind. An involuntary yelp escaped my throat. I felt vulnerable, like I was the thing being shot at.

The pounding in the ground felt like a rapid heartbeat, and I thought for a moment it was my own. Then I heard it; the bull crashed through the trees and stopped only a few yards from me. He stared at me wildly, wall-eyed, his nostrils flaring; the dense paddles of his gigantic antlers looked like instant destruction or death to anything that might lie in the path of this twelve hundred pound, fury-on-the-hoof beast. I shrank back, attempting to hide behind the nearest trees, and held my breath. Nothing. No sound, no movement for, seemingly, an eternity.

Finally, I felt, more than heard, the moose trot away from me on down the hill. I released the trapped air in my lungs and gasped for a fresh breath as I watched him veer to the west. Cal came panting through the alders on his wild chase, rifle held at the ready, pointed forward and down, like he was on patrol again in a Vietnamese jungle.

Relieved to see him, I stepped out from behind the trees. He whirled in my direction, swinging the rifle up. "Hey, it's me!" I shouted, pointing at the gun.

"Oh, sorry." He lowered the gun and shot rapid glances around. "Did you see him? Which way did he go?"

I pointed down the hill, and without saying another word, Cal lurched away. I was suddenly amused, thinking how comical he looked, all hunkered over as he was, creeping along with long strides, feet splayed, his heels set down slowly, the toes following with exaggerated stealth, the rifle again pointing straight ahead.

I turned downhill and followed—at a slower pace—the hunter and the hunted. I felt pretty certain that the animal was safe, at least for this night. When I reached the valley floor, I headed back to camp and had a can of stew bubbling on the gas stove by the time Cal came trudging in. He rifled around in the cooler and brought out a beer, pulled the tab, and sighed as the can hissed foam over the edge. He drank deeply before speaking. "Well, by God, that was him, I know it! I'll get him tomorrow."

During the night the wind rose, and our tent flapped in an ever-increasing gale. I heard waves slapping the shore, and when I got up to relieve myself I realized how chill the air had become. Zero, or thereabouts, was my guess, judging from the crystalline feeling in my nostrils as I inhaled.

An aurora borealis streaked the clear sky with blues and greens. I watched gauzy fingers of vapor lift and drape, fold and waver, fade and burst again with color. An electrical hum filled the air with ethereal music, and I watched the display until the cold became intolerable. When I returned to the tent I woke Cal to share it with him. But, he only grunted something about needing his sleep—said he could see the "blankety-blank" Northern Lights any time, and for me to shut up and go to sleep. He turned again to his slumber. With a fresh sense of unease and loneliness, I crawled deep into my cocoon to try to stay warm.

The night dragged by; sleep refused to come to a mind kept alert, ears listening for any foreign sound or movement. And it seemed that nature was more than willing to oblige my paranoia, because frequently during the night I imagined footfalls, crackling brush, grunts and snorts, and I'd strain every muscle to listen. Just before dawn a wolf howled somewhere off in the distance, and I shuddered involuntarily at the eerie sound.

Finally in exhaustion, I fell into a deep pre-dawn sleep. I dreamed I was being chased—by the wolf? A moose? A bear? I woke in a sweat, shaking and breathless. I heard Cal's dry hacking cough; he was already up, clattering cooking utensils. The scent of coffee drew me out of the tent.

"I think we'll go the other way across the river valley and try the north bank this morning," he said. "Then, this afternoon, if we haven't had any luck, I'll try up on the other ridge, where we saw him last night." We ate breakfast hurriedly, without talking. I could see Cal was already mentally in search of the big moose.

The first several river channels were shallow and narrow so I was able to ford them in my hiking boots without getting my feet wet. But the last crossing seemed to be the main channel, too far across and too deep. Cal put on his hip waders and carried our packs and his rifle across, depositing them on the other bank, before returning for me.

I'd drenched myself in insect repellent before dressing, and I was secretly pleased to see the mosquitoes were bothering Cal instead of me. He slapped at a horde of them circling his head, but if they bit him I couldn't tell, because he gave no sign.

"Climb on my back," he instructed as he squatted before me. "Put your arms around my neck." I did as he said, wondering if he really could handle my weight, not that it is all that considerable, compared to his large, muscular frame.

He took a couple of steps along the solid bank, to get the feel and balance, before stepping into the water. The flow of water was sluggish and slow, but due to the glacial content, the bottom could not be seen, requiring each step be taken gingerly and carefully.

"Hold your feet up," he panted as the water climbed up the legs of his hip waders. I lifted them higher and tightened my grip around his neck. I could feel him struggle for foot control, as well as for breath. The crossing seemed like a slow-motion movie. The only sounds were the shushing flow of the river, a silvery-tinkle of ice crystals shattering along the edge where the water had frozen, Cal's ragged breathing, and the pounding of my heart. I noticed white puffs of his exhaled air; they seemed to float ghost-like from his mouth, hovering, then wafting away over the flow of water, like an ominous warning—the autumn of his breath, slowly giving way to winter death.

When at last we reached solid ground, Cal pushed me off his back, before flopping down in a heap. I dropped beside him; we looked at each other and giggled, giddy with relief that we were both still dry.

"Hey, about last night...you know...about my Ruger and all..." he stammered. He reached out to touch my bruised cheek. "I'm sorry. It's just that it cost so much," he continued. Then when he saw my expression, he said, "Not that you aren't more valuable." A look—one almost of tenderness— swept across his face and for a brief instant I felt like I would cry. It'd been so long since he looked at me like that.

"Forgive me?" he asked.

I touched his hand, still resting against my cheek. "I forgive you," I said.

He removed his hand then and as he started to stand, he bent and lightly kissed the spot. He cleared his throat, as if embarrassed. "Well, let's get on with the hunt," he said brightly, apparently feeling his burden of guilt suddenly lifted.

He stashed the waders under a bush near the water's edge and we adjusted our loads, preparing for the hike ahead.

Cal carried the rifle over his shoulder, a set of binoculars around his neck, and his .357 Ruger holstered on his hip. He also carried our "survival" gear in his backpack, along with dry set of clothes, and bags to hold the heart and liver of our game, if we were fortunate enough to bag the beast. In my pack I carried our lunch and snack foods, more emergency supplies, and my extra set of clothes. We each had our own drinking water.

The sun had just come over the horizon—the late-autumn air crisp—when we started up a game trail skirting the river floor below. Here the underbrush was spongy, as I suspected it might be—a muskeg bog that hid downed tree trunks and pockets of water, making it hard to traverse. We were in the open and could see up and down the valley. Cal pointed out that we could even see our camp from here. We were both quiet, each mesmerized by the morning and lost in our own thoughts.

By noon we had covered several miles, working our way deeper up the drainage, and when we stopped for lunch, we were again in a heavy stand of alders. As during the walk the evening before, the trees had scratched any bare skin surface available to their nasty clawing. Our progress was made even worse by the packs on our backs. I was tired and not happy. Cal was in a sour mood too, because we'd not seen any encouraging signs of his quarry.

We ate in silence, both sullen and cold. "Well," he said, finally, "I guess we ought to start working our way back."

"Let's rest a while longer before we go. Please," I implored him. "I'm beat."

He'd already hoisted his pack on. A look that I couldn't quite understand crossed his face. Was it anger? Disgust? Frustration? "Okay, I'll give you another fifteen minutes," he said. "We've got a long ways to go to get back to camp, and I want to be set up and waiting on that other ridge before dusk, just in case he comes back that way tonight."

He took off his pack again and leaned it against one of the standing alders, then dropped down beside it. He mumbled something as he did so, and when I asked what he'd said, he barked, "I just said I should've left you in camp, that's all."

We returned pretty much the way we'd come, except that we climbed a little higher up the ridge, so as to be more camouflaged against the edge of the trees. Cal led, of course, setting a pace I wasn't comfortable with, making me feel pressured and rushed. It made me mad, and I walked along swearing under my breath, wishing I hadn't agreed to come with him on this horrid trip.

After a couple of hours of hard tramping we reached an area covered with blueberries—hundreds of plants pressed low to the ground, bearing ripe, purple fruit. I sank down, and casting my pack aside, I greedily began to pluck the small, firm fruit, stuffing them into my mouth at once. It was the moisture I sought, as much as the flavor.

I didn't care that Cal had tramped right on through the bushes—I was going to rest here and eat my fill. I looked up just in time to see him disappearing around a bend and, instead of feeling anxious, I was surprised to feel a sudden rush of relief—like my jailer wasn't watching and I'd been allowed to escape, if only for a few moments.

We were within a mile or so of camp, and I knew I could find my own way back without any problem. I'd have to ford the deepest channel of the river, but I could change into dry clothes shortly after, when I reached camp.

And so I indulged myself and, from a reclining position, wallowed in the berry patch, eating the tasty little berries to my heart's content. After I'd had my fill, I stretched out on my back and let the afternoon sun send its sweet warmth down onto my tired body. It made me drowsy and I dozed off.

A half an hour must have gone by before I heard the gun shot, followed by that terrible sound. How I wish now that I could blot that hideous screech from my memory. It had to have come from him, but it sounded so otherworldly that I still find it hard to accept that it was a human voice! Was that my name being screamed? It tore through me like a jagged, blunt sword, ripping a hole in my soul that will never be repaired.

I leaped to my feet, struggled into my pack and ran as fast as I could over the squatty berry plants until I came to a crude game trail. I plunged along it until I reached the point where I'd last seen Cal. Nothing was in sight, so I sped ahead in the direction I assumed he'd gone.

The game trail plowed into a thicket of alder, and ignoring their grasping branches, I struggled through them, oblivious to the fresh scratches on my exposed skin. I heard sounds of a struggle from somewhere ahead—human screams and a hideous bestial gnarling, snapping branches and thrashing brush, and more agonizing cries. I raced on, trying to cover the intervening distance as quickly as possible. As I ran, sobbing and burning with fear, the alarmed cries came less frequently... fading...fading...a final gasp, then silence.

Suddenly I was in a clearing—another blueberry patch—and what I saw made my heart stop and my blood freeze. Oh, my God, help us, I prayed. A huge grizzly stood over my husband, one front paw in the middle of his back, its sharp teeth in the nape of Cal's neck. As I watched, the beast rose up onto its hind legs and swung its great, fierce head from side to side, looking in all directions. I instinctively dropped to the ground and crawled behind a bush. I was far enough away I doubted it'd seen me, but I know a bear's sense of smell is incredibly sharp.

What to do now, I thought frantically! I peered through the shrubbery, horrified, not wanting to, yet unable to keep from looking. I desperately watched for some sign of life in Cal, but he lay absolutely still, except when the bear pulled at him. Perhaps, I thought, he is doing as they advise— playing dead. I dared not move, myself, until the bear had been satisfied that its prey was completely inert. I knew it probably would move off a ways to wait for its intended meal to "ripen." Our only hope was that the beast would leave soon.

At long last I saw the bear nudge Cal with its snout, then begin to walk into the woods. It turned once, as if not quite yet satisfied, and bounced back, barking its unique "woof," again pouncing on Cal's back with both front feet. Then, with a satisfied grunt it finally paced away, and I lost sight of it as it disappeared in the trees.

I lay still for several more minutes before I cautiously stood and warily crept to the sight of the carnage. It took all the nerve I could muster. I dropped my pack near his where he'd apparently discarded it in his attempt at flight. His rifle was close by him, probably knocked out of his hands in the initial attack. His right hand was under him, as if he'd been trying to get the pistol out of its holster.

Before touching him, I knew he was dead. Blood stained his shirt and jeans crimson; his hat, soaked with blood and bear slobber, lay crumpled in a wad on the ground beside his mutilated head. I could see where the scalp had been torn away, leaving the skull bare and exposed. His ear, attached to the flap of scalp, now lay on his shoulder.

The smell of blood, urine, feces, and the stench of bear made we wretch and I emptied my stomach. The blueberries I'd so greedily eaten, now wasted in a puddle of vomit, made me feel guilty and unclean. If only I'd stayed with him... perhaps he'd still be alive. Great wracking waves of grief poured from my throat, black and sour. I knelt in the gore, rocked back and forth, tearing at my hair, and gave myself over to the shrill keening that happened on its own.

The sun was beginning to drop behind the ridge before I was able to get control of my emotions. I calmed down and started to study the situation. I had to try to find a way to carry his shredded body back to our camp.

But, then suddenly I heard snapping branches coming from the timber. Fear for my own safety bolted me into action. A flush started between my shoulder blades, quickly spread up my neck, and the fine hairs on my face stood erect, prickling my cheeks. I snatched up my pack and grabbed the rifle as I bolted from the area, heading directly to the river. I know better than to try to outrun a bear, but I also knew that my only chance was to put as much distance between me and the danger before it came back for its kill. And, so I ran, blindly, desperately, without any other thought than saving my life.

I splashed through the deepest channel, thoroughly soaking myself to the waist, but I didn't pay any attention to it. Once on the other side, I turned to look back, and thankfully, saw nothing. I stumbled ahead, turning directly towards camp, skirting the clumps of brush that stood in the way. Every so often I looked behind me, but saw I was not being pursued. I didn't slacken my pace, however, wanting to reach the relative safety of camp. What safety was that, really? It was only a small tent on an open beach, at the edge of the water where animals come to drink.

As I rounded a larger stand of willows, only a few hundred yards from camp, I saw it standing there—the bull moose of Cal's dreams. I was tempted to shoot it myself—for Cal, who would never have the opportunity again. But, common sense kept me from venting my rage at this innocent animal. The scent of fresh animal blood was not something I needed in my camp. It suddenly hit me—"my camp." I'm alone.

The moose, startled by my presence, bolted away, looking as wild-eyed as he had the night before.

That was the longest night in the history of my forty years on this earth. I built a huge fire and kept it blazing all night, hoping it would keep all the predators away, including my own dark thoughts. Kept awake by my fears of being attacked in the night, and the awful thought of my husband—his flesh perhaps, even at that moment, feeding the bear—out there in the dark, I could only pray. I prayed, rather selfishly it seems to me now, for my own safety. I prayed for Cal's soul. I prayed for forgiveness for being angry with him so often. I prayed for my dear children, snug in their beds, not knowing their father would never be coming home again. I prayed for strength to go back to the sight of the slaughter tomorrow, to try to gather what I could of him to bring him home.

The night passed without a wink of sleep, and I felt dazed and numb when I arose in the morning. I automatically looked across the valley, searching—irrationally hoping—to see Cal coming towards me, but of course I saw nothing.

After the sun began to warm the earth, I started back across the river valley. I reached the dreaded area after cautiously approaching from the bank of the river where, this time, I'd stripped off my jeans to keep them dry during the crossing. But, there was no evidence left of the awful killing that happened only a few hours before. If I hadn't located his pack, I wouldn't have known for sure that this was the site. Cal's body was gone, clothes and all. I was horrified, and frantically searched the clearing. Drag marks, and bear prints—one set of very large ones, the claws extending way ahead of the toes, and several smaller ones, looking like one, or perhaps two, cubs.

A sow with spring cubs! Cal had probably come upon them, accidentally, as they fed on the blueberries, and she had done what any mother would do—protected her young.

I followed the grisly trail until it disappeared into the thick timber. Fear of falling victim to a similar fate kept me from entering the dark woods to pursue further. I could only go back to camp and wait for Clint to return in his plane to pick me up.

Those two days of waiting are now but a nightmarish blur. Clint seemed understanding and sympathetic at first, but now I know it was he who cast doubt and suspicion on me. I apparently have him to thank for my recent torture.

Oh, yes. Of course, they sent people to investigate—men with tracking skills and men with weapons that could handle a murderous bear. But they returned without a shred of evidence, shaking their heads saying, "It was possible that she's telling the truth,"—there were obvious bear signs in the general area. Yet, curiously, there were no remains to be found—no blood, no bones, no clothing, not even the crumpled hat. They all looked at me with doubting eyes. Had I killed him, thrown his body in the lake maybe, or found a deep hole in the river? My motive? There was, after all, that stupid remark. Clint's mention of it in his report was all it took.

Epilogue: After the trial, she took her two children and left Alaska, never intending to return again. The jury found her not guilty of the murder of her husband, due to lack of convincing evidence—or any evidence. She now lives in obscurity in a small town in the Midwest.

Shared Solitude

It was the silence that David loved about this place. The solitude to be had in his remote Alaska backwoods home brought him peace. He'd gone last August to visit his brother in Los Angeles, and the city noises had driven him crazy in two short weeks.

"How can you stand to be alone way out there in the woods by yourself for months on end?" Caroline, his brother's wife, had asked.

She looked bewildered when he responded, "How can you possibly stand living in this concrete jungle?"

He liked Caroline. A lot. She was a sensible woman, stronger than his brother, Delbert. Smarter, too. Delbert, two years younger than David, had suffered with asthma from early childhood and because of his frail condition, everyone had coddled him. He was smart enough, to be sure. He'd studied hard, had finally gotten his CPA license, and now was a partner in a well-known accounting firm—had a corner office on the tenth floor of the Occidental Building downtown.

But the fact remained that the two brothers never had anything in common—nothing beyond their dark hair and a little indentation in their square chins.

David now stood looking from the south window of his snug log cabin, sipping strong black coffee, his thoughts on his brother's wife. Actually, he hadn't thought of much of anything else since receiving her letter a couple of weeks ago.

It would be sunny in Los Angeles today. He could imagine her—long tan legs in white shorts, a brightly colored band around her auburn hair—getting into her silver Volvo and driving to the tennis court to meet her friends for a morning of exercise. Later they would probably all have lunch at that little sandwich shop where she'd taken him the day before he'd left to come home. She would probably have her usual avocado and sprout sandwich on stone ground bread and maybe carrot juice. It was during that lunch that she had placed her smooth warm hand on his bare forearm, looked deep into his eyes with her own green ones, and had asked him that question.

"You must get terribly lonely," she said. "Why don't you find a nice girl and get married?"

In response he'd only shrugged. Then he asked her the question that had been plaguing him. "Are you and Delbert happy?"

For a long moment she looked down at her meal, playing with the fresh vegetables, arranging them to form a funny face on her plate—black olive eyes, celery hair, and a stern straight carrot mouth. Before answering his question, she pulled a few sprouts from her sandwich, made a curly mustache on the upper lip, and then looked up at him laughing. "It's not as trim as yours," she said. "I think it might be nice if Delbert grew one. But he says it wouldn't be appropriate for someone in his position, whatever that means."

He waited for her to answer his question, knowing her well enough by now to realize that it was easier for her to make a joke than to let her real feelings be known—to anyone, except maybe him.

"We're okay," she finally said. "I sometimes wish he were more like you. He's so uptight, so engrossed in making it up the corporate ladder. I guess he thinks he has a lot to prove to everyone—mostly himself. You were always the capable one." She stroked his arm again with perfectly polished fingernails. "The one with all the looks and brains and muscles." He knew she was flirting with him.

She grew more serious. "Your brother is good to me and I have a great life. I'm very happy. Really."

David wasn't convinced. He hadn't seen anything resembling happiness from either of them in the two weeks he'd been there.

"Let's talk about you," she said, changing the subject. She moved her hand from his arm to his knee. "So explain to me why you are such a loner. Are you gay or something?" She grinned, knowing that remark would get to him.

He felt his ears begin to warm. Was it from her remark or from her touch? It had to be his response to her hand on his leg. They both knew he wasn't gay.

He tried to remember that touch now as he stood looking across the lake, frozen since the middle of October. It was now late into January. The pelts from the animals he'd caught on his trap line had surpassed those of the past seven seasons. They were especially thick this year and he expected to realize a good return for the winter's work.

It had snowed again yesterday and most of the night. He loved the delicious stillness of a world swaddled in fresh-fallen snow. The mounds of snow on his wood chopping block reminded him of Caroline's breasts below her tan line— full, soft, and white but, unlike the snow, warm.

They'd made love only once—a brief release from their unique brands of loneliness—on that last afternoon. Tenderly, affectionately, with a purity and simplicity that left him feeling no guilt, even though she belonged to his own brother.

The weather had cleared this morning. The first rays of an arctic sun pierced through thick stands of scrubby pine across the thumb of the lake. The lake was roughly in the shape of Lower Michigan—a flat hand held face up, with the thumb slightly extended away from the rest, creating a protected cove. He'd built his cabin near the end of the thumb at the edge of a clearing, a short distance from a smooth sandy beach. From his window he could see all of the lake except for the "fingers" out of sight beyond a wooded peninsula. The main lake was deep, making the broad "palm" an easy place for landing the bush plane that came with his mail and supplies twice a month. In fact, he expected Clint to show up any day now. He knew he should have an answer to Caroline's letter ready to send back with Clint, but he still didn't know what to say.

David refilled his cup and returned to the window. He touched the rough burlap makeshift curtains and thought of the lacy yellow ones in Caroline's kitchen back in California.

He imagined himself there, watching her at work mixing batter or poaching eggs. He was feeling melancholy this morning—the long hours of darkness and cold were wearing on his nerves. Even so, he knew he wouldn't have his life any other way.

He watched shy tendrils of early sunlight touch the frozen lake with golden rays. Then he saw a movement, a dark form across the lake. In that shaft of light—then moving behind that tree, then closer—disappearing, then reappearing through another sliver of sun—the animal roved through the timber. Finally it turned to face the cabin. The wolf had first shown up just before Thanksgiving, always staying to the southern shore of the lake. It had been missing several days now—maybe a week or more, and David had supposed the *lobo* had gone for good.

The first time he'd seen it he was returning from checking his traps. His dogs had suddenly stopped, nearly mid-stride, causing him to collide with the sled. In the woods across the thumb stood a lone timber wolf, silent as death, staring calmly from the shadows. There was something eerie about the green eyes fixed upon him. It was an unusually large animal—dark gray, almost black. David estimated at the shoulder it would be as tall as his kitchen table and probably weighed 150 pounds.

His first instinct as a hunter, of course, was to shoot it, but something in those eyes stopped him. Man and wolf had observed each other over several weeks from the safety of the frozen lake between them. Nearly every morning the wolf appeared in the shadows for a time, staring unabashedly across at the cabin before vanishing quietly into the woods.

Sometimes, on a clear morning like this one, David would slip on his coat, walk outside with his coffee and lean against the side of the cabin to let the animal know it was being observed, as well. Once he'd walked down the slope of beach toward the wolf to see what it would do. It did not turn immediately away as might have been expected, nor did it show any agitation. Instead, it sat on its haunches and watched David intently. They remained so, studying one another for fifteen minutes. David was the one to weary of their game first and turn back to the cabin. But then the animal had disappeared. Seeing it again now, he felt as if an old friend had returned. He whistled cheerfully as he prepared for his trip to check his traps.

Before he left the cabin his eyes fell again on Caroline's letter lying on the table. He put it in an inside pocket and planned to mentally compose an answer while he ran his route.

David started at the north end of the loop, easily working his way along the entire trap line in his customary two-day time. The catch was exceedingly good. The crates attached to his sled were nearly full—several hares and an ermine in the smaller one, a beaver and an otter in another, two white arctic foxes in the third. The trip had gone smoothly and he was on the south side of the loop an hour earlier than expected. He had reached his last trap—only two miles from his cabin—and he was anxious to get home and have a hot meal. After a night's sleep in his warm bed he'd start skinning the animals in the morning, so the pelts could begin curing.

A deep ravine, gouged down the mountainside by spring thaws, crossed under the trail. Several large logs lay across the cut, forming a bridge. The drainage was filled with heavy brush, downed timber, rocks and forest debris, making it an ideal habitat for small animals. He usually had something in this trap, often a snowshoe hare. It only required a quick stop and he could generally count on having fried rabbit for supper.

David halted the team, draped the lines across the back of the sled, and without taking time to set the brake, he started up the bank to check his trap. But something was different. He couldn't find the trap! The circle of ground around the stake holding it was scraped clean by the drag-chain. Beyond this circle tundra had been ripped into shreds. He was puzzled. There was no sound or movement.

Suddenly, without warning, a ferocious mass sprang from the thicket—snarling, hissing, plunging—hitting David squarely in the chest. The chain checked the attack and flung the animal to the ground. A wolverine's heavy body dropped with a sharp thud at the trapper's feet. It snarled and recoiled, preparing to strike again. There was a look of frenzy in its wide-set eyes. Sharp yellow teeth bared menacingly, long curved claws dug into the soil for traction.

David momentarily froze in surprise, but then he stumbled backwards across the log bridge, as the animal sprang again. He slipped and fell over the edge, forgetting in his fright, that the trail dropped immediately into the deep drainage.

As he tumbled into the ravine, the tips of his snowshoes caught under the edge of the bridge, trapping and suspending both legs. His body crashed, head first, into the brush and rocks below, where he landed on his back, both legs held fast above him. He heard an eerie cracking sound and at first thought the log had broken from the stress of his weight. But the screaming pain in his right leg told a more frightening story.

He lay still, gasping for breath, trying to replace the wind that had been knocked from him. He grit his teeth and clenched his eyes so tightly he saw stars. He was oblivious to other bruising in his body, only aware of the extreme agony in his broken leg. He tried to free himself but, after repeated efforts, realized his snowshoes were impossibly wedged under the log; he was completely incapacitated—caught in a trap of his own carelessness. Only the rough, rocky washout under the weight of his torso kept him from dangling like a caught salmon at the end of a fishing line.

He was vaguely aware of his team yelping wildly in confusion, then of soft schussing sounds as they dragged the sled away down trail. The yaps of his dogs gradually became thin and wavering in the distance, leaving him alone and completely vulnerable in the wilderness

Then he heard something truly frightening—a relentless clatter of the metal trap smashing against the rocks a few short feet away. If the wolverine freed itself, or if the drag-chain didn't hold, the fierce beast could kill him. He was absolutely defenseless.

Long shadows bent towards the lake, as he lay in this condition, unable to move his lower body. The time it takes for winter evenings to become total darkness in the far north is brief and soon he couldn't see.

Time crept slowly by. Pain dulled all other physical sensations, but his mind was as sharp and clear as the points of stars piercing the black arctic night sky above him. As he gazed into that sky, his mind wandered, imagining how it might feel to be a lone astronaut, lost in space, circling the earth for an eternity in endless revolutions—round and round and round—with no hope of rescue. With that kind of acuity he realized just how fragile life is—how totally alone and vulnerable he was at that moment.

His logical mind took over, pushing away the sense of panic lurking there. How long had it been since Clint came with mail and supplies? A couple of weeks at least. Yes, in fact, the letter in his pocket had arrived exactly two weeks ago, even though it had been posted from LA two weeks before that and had sat in the post office waiting until Clint's next bush run. That meant that if the weather held, Clint could be expected within the next day or two.

David calculated that in this condition he might survive that long, maybe a little longer, but not much beyond that. It would likely hit thirty degrees below zero before late morning sun brought the mercury back up. He was well protected with the layers of arctic clothing he had on, but he didn't know how long his extremities could survive without being flexed. He beat his arms together and shifted his upper body as much as he could under the constraining circumstances.

His sleep was sporadic and fitful throughout the long night. His dreams were tormented and troubling. Once he woke to a deathly stillness, all except for the familiar ethereal humming of the aurora borealis. He looked up and saw them—filmy fingers swirling like illuminated fronds of vapor—blue and green, white and red.

The silence was broken by the sound of an animal crawling away through the trees. David recognized the sound as being that of the wolverine, probably now missing one gnawed-off leg, dragging its body slowly up the ravine away from him. He felt relieved.

Later, the howl of a wolf came from somewhere near the lake. He thought of his dogs, shackled by the sled, probably in a hopeless tangle of lines, standing defenseless somewhere. David hoped they were, at least, at the cabin. And he hoped the wolf would leave them alone. They were nearly as vulnerable as he was.

When at long last light began to flicker through the trees, he slept again. He dreamed of Caroline. She was kneeling beside him, wearing a flowing gown of white, gardenias woven into her auburn hair. Her lips felt cool as she kissed his forehead, the sensation lingering even after she pulled back. He smiled into her green eyes and then frowned as her image evaporated like a mist melting in sunlight. He awoke, and in that semi-wakeful state he touched the spot where he'd felt her lips, still sensing the coolness. A film of frost had formed there.

With the image of her clearly in his mind, he slowly opened his own eyes and was startled by what he saw. It jolted him into full awareness. A pair of green eyes was, unwaveringly, staring back at him—not the tender, soft ones belonging to Caroline, as in his dream, but large, intense, canine eyes.

The black wolf stood on the bridge above him, fixing him with a steady gaze. Now, instead of the chill of frost on his cheeks, he felt hot, flushed, as blood began to pound

through his veins. He realized the grave danger he was in—
the trapper in a trap. As a trapper, David knew, full well, that
untold dangers lurk just out of sight here in the remote frozen
north. Yet he never expected that he might become the prey.
With clarity, he knew that this could be his time to die.

He'd never feared being alone, had never feared death.
Even now, knowing his life was at stake either from the wolf
or the elements, he was not afraid. But if he had a choice
between the two possible deaths, he supposed he would rather
it be the latter. Being eaten alive wouldn't be his preference.

"I should have killed you long ago. Don't know why I
didn't." He spoke softly to his friend and foe. "Well, old boy,
guess you've got the advantage now." He waited for the attack
that was bound to come.

For several moments man and wolf warily watched
each other. Then, surprisingly, the wolf turned to face down
the trail leading towards David's cabin. He sat down on his
haunches as if waiting, ears pricked, an intense expression in
the unblinking eyes. A few minutes passed before the animal
stood, turned in a complete circle, walked again to the edge of
the ravine and stared over the edge at David, giving him
another meaningful look, and then quickly disappeared into
the timber.

David was still looking after the wolf, watching the
dark spot in the woods where it had gone, when he heard
sounds coming from the trail. He recognized the din of his
own dogs' excited barks, and through the racket, Clint's voice
encouraging them.

"Thank God," David whispered. His lips felt stiff and
unnatural when he moved them. As they got closer he tried

to get Clint's attention. "I'm here," he rasped, knowing even as he said the words that they had not reached much further than his own mouth. He cleared his throat and spoke again, forcing the sound up the gulch, hoping to be heard on the trail overhead.

Moments later the pilot was beside him. "Christ-a-mighty, man. What happened?" Clint scrambled down the bank. "Damned good to see you're alive. Had me scared half out of my mind—your empty cabin, the dog team in disarray, still tied to the sled and looking mighty pitiful. Didn't think I'd ever get them mangy mutts untangled."

When David struggled to speak, his tongue felt like cracked leather on a pair of hiking boots badly in need of oil. Clint grasped the situation and pulled a bottle of water from his pack. Lifting David's head he helped his friend drink, then carefully began to unfasten the snowshoes. "Good lord, how long have you been here like this?" he asked. "Where are you hurt?"

"My right leg. Happened yesterday afternoon." David groaned in pain.

Clint gingerly felt along David's shinbone until he found the bone protruding. "Oh, Christ!" Clint exclaimed. "I'm afraid this is going to hurt, buddy. Sorry, but I've got to get these snowshoes off." He cut the bindings with his knife and carefully pulled them off.

David grit his teeth, wincing with fresh pain as Clint freed his legs and helped lower them to the ground.

"We've got to get you to the hospital fast," Clint said. He looked around for something to use as a splint. "This'll work," he said, grabbing one of the snowshoes.

He began cutting the webbing away and broke the frame into four lengths of smooth strong wood. "Strangest thing just happened," he said as he worked, shaking his head as if trying to understand. "Just as we reached the end of the lake, a big black wolf loped out of the trees, nearly scaring the team into fits. He stood watching us until I got them back under control, and then he raced on ahead of us up the trail."

Clint placed the wooden supports around David's leg and bound them into place with the webbing. "He was sitting right here waiting on the bridge when the team rounded the bend. It was almost like he was showing me where you were," he continued. "Damnedest thing I've ever seen. Wouldn't have believed it if I hadn't seen it myself."

Several hours later David was resting in the hospital, his leg in traction. The painkillers had allowed him to sleep some and now, after a hot meal, he was feeling much better. He leaned back against the pillows and read Caroline's letter again—words he'd read so often he nearly had them memorized.

My Dearest David,

Much has happened since you were here. I should have written before this, but have waited until there was a definiteness to some issues, one of which involves you.

Delbert and I have decided to get a divorce—the grounds merely "Irreconcilable differences." I suspect you will not be surprised, for you obviously questioned our happiness. I wonder if you knew more than you let on, but even if you did, it's not important now. We have agreed to a fair and amicable settlement, an easy thing to do, I suppose, for two people who neither love nor hate each other, and the papers have already been filed. I will move out of the house in a couple of months when everything is final.

If you're not sitting down, you should be when I tell you the next piece of news. How I wish I could tell you in person to help soften the blow. I am pregnant. I have managed to keep it a secret from everyone until now—including Delbert. I've especially not told him for he would immediately know the truth. The child is not his. He is sterile. Were you aware of that?

I wonder what you must be thinking right now, David. Yes, you are the father of the child I have carried for these five months. My condition is becoming apparent and, of course, he will need to be told soon. However, I promise to protect your identity so the two of you can maintain a brotherly relationship.

I am not unhappy about the turn of events. I used to wish I could have a baby, but gave that dream up long ago. Then I was glad there were no children in our emotionally empty home. I had a resurgence of happiness when you were here, and yes, even love. In those brief moments we shared, David, I felt more love than I've known in a very long time. I realize our two worlds are as far apart as any two worlds could ever be. Living in a city would be your death and I don't know if I could adapt to a solitary life, such as yours, yet I am willing to try. I want to be with you when I deliver

my child—our child. May I come? Please don't deny me.
I anxiously await your answer.

Love,
Caroline

At last David felt he was ready with his answer. He reached for the paper and pen on the bedside table and began to write.

Dear Caroline,

When I read your letter, I was again grateful for the solitude of my wilderness home. I've been unable to think of much else, beyond your astounding news. If I lived where I had to interact with people while I absorbed it all I don't know how well I would have been able to handled it. I know you have been waiting for an answer—anxiously, no doubt— but it's taken me this long to sort out my feelings.

Knowing Delbert as I do, I was not surprised about the news of your divorce. He's always been overly competitive and never learned how to successfully handle personal relationships, including one with me. I'm happy you have been able to settle the business affairs agreeably, hopefully without too much pain to either of you.

During the past two weeks I think I've experienced every emotion in the book about your news that I am to be a father. Even writing the word now seems foreign and strange, almost sacrilegious. I've never considered what it would be like to have a son—or daughter—of my own. That idea has been as remote to me (but not nearly as frightening) as living in a big city. Yet, the image of a little tyke following me around calling me 'daddy' has a strange appeal.

There shouldn't be any doubt that I've always cared for you. And knowing that you will soon to be the mother of my child makes my feelings for you even stronger. The memory of that last afternoon is still fresh in my mind. It seemed so right, so perfect, and I've had no regrets. How can it be possible, I ask myself, that one brief liaison could produce such long lasting effects? Yet, here is evidence that destiny is sometimes beyond our control. We will deal with it.

You are correct in saying city living would not suit me. But, a current event has made me realize that even my solitary way of life has its downfalls. As I write I am lying in the hospital, lucky to have survived a wilderness accident, a story that might well have had a different ending, if not for fate's intervention. It's just a broken leg that will mend. But, as I waited for help to come, I gave a lot of thought to the benefits of living in town.

It's only a small town but it's filled with good and caring people. It is near enough to my cabin that I can commute when I need to. I do worry that if you come here, you'll miss the full social life you're accustomed to. And I know that at times I'll miss living in the peace and quiet of my cabin on the lake. It would be a big step and adjustment for both of us. Yet, if you think you'd like to give it a try, I'm willing. There is a good doctor here and I know of a house that is available that would be suitable for a small family. (How strange that word sounds to me—yet at the same time,

how appealing.)
    Write and let me know what your decision is.
                                    Lovingly,
                                        David

The small plane bobbed in shallow water at the edge of the lake as Clint loaded the final boxes being taken to the house in town. David, with the aid of one crutch, hopped to where Caroline stood watching. With his free hand he patted her expanding belly, then put his arm around her. Clint joined them and the three stood silently looking across the water, reluctant to leave the peaceful scene. The late afternoon sunlight, shining among the trees on the point of land across the thumb from the cabin, created long shadows.

Suddenly two animals emerged and loped along the opposite shoreline. "That's him," Clint whispered, "that's the wolf that met me on the trail and showed me where you were." The big male wolf paused and turned to face them. He cast a long glance towards the cabin, then turned to look after the other smaller wolf—apparently his new mate. He loped off after her, disappearing into the dark woods.

"Yes, that is him," David said. "I see he's not alone anymore either." He smiled at Clint, and saw him shaking his head, as if still in disbelief.

"I'm glad he has someone to share his solitude with," he said as he helped Caroline into the plane. He kissed her gently. "As for me, I believe my solitude is a thing of the past." He suddenly realized he was very happy.

Two Thumbs Up

Jo Massey

The chain of events leading up to my death begins right after work last Friday night. I go, as is my custom, to Chilcoot Charlie's out on the Highway. The bartender cashes my paycheck, sets me up with a beer, and I wander over to join a bunch of oil field roughnecks playing liar's poker with dollar bills. We play out a few hands and drink a few more beers.

After a while, this one guy gets the bright idea of playing with twenties. "Well, okay," says I. "Just one time." I have a real good hand, a winning hand, and I know it. I start to reach for their twenties when one of them says, "Hey, Bud, this number beats yours," and his friends all agree with him. I know it's not true and I say so. "Pay up, asshole," he yells. So I say, "hell no," and something like "get screwed" and I leave. Then these guys all burst out the door behind me and by instinct, I pull my jackknife out of its sheath and stand there, facing them, hunched down, ready to spring.

Well, there's four of them, see, and just one of me. They all four jump on me, throwing me to the ground. One big guy lays himself across my legs so I can't move while two of the others grab my arms and wrestle my knife away from me. They hold me all stretched out like they were going to gut me like a deer, and then the next thing you know, the fourth guy, the big ugly one with a jagged scar on his cheek, stretches out my right thumb and whacks it off with my own knife. Then he whacks off my left thumb. Sonofabitch! That hurt like hell! They all haul off and kick me hard with their steel-toed boots and swagger back into the bar, laughing and slapping each other on the back.

I lay there kind of dazed like, until I see the blood pumping out the end of where my thumbs used to be. Well, I'm hurting bad see, and bleeding all over everywhere, so I go home and wrap some big bandages on the stumps to stop the bleeding. No easy task, let me tell you! I learn real quick how handy thumbs can be. But a couple of chugs on a bottle of Jack Daniels helps kill some of the pain.

All the time I'm getting madder and madder thinking about what these guys did to me and I figure it's time someone taught them a lesson. I take down my shotgun and fill my coat pockets with double ought buck. Then I jump into my old half-ton Jimmy and start driving up the highway looking for them.

They aren't at Chilcoot's anymore, so I go on to Shorty's Bar. From the number of cars in the parking lot, it looks like everybody in town is here. Good. I'll make them crawl in front of all these folks. Sure enough, I walk in and there's old Scarface in the middle of a bunch of oilies telling them his version of the story and laughing about how they'd really fixed me.

He's saying, "What do you reckon the ol' bastard'll find to do for a living now? Won't be able to climb them power poles any more!"

The big guy with him says, "I reckon this'll be the end of his huntin' and fishin', too. That'll kill him. I hear tell that's all he lives for now that his old lady ran off with Sly."

"Yeah, but worse'n that he's gonna have to start wearing girlie pants. See, you can't hardly work your zipper without thumbs," Scarface says, and he pretends to try to undo his own right there. Everyone is laughing hard by now. Then this big ugly goon and his buddy propose a toast to me and lift their glasses high over everyone's heads and clink them together. "Wait," says Scarface and he picks my thumbs up off the table and flips one into each of their glasses like they were olives in a martini. "Thumbs up," he says, "Hell, two thumbs up," and they toss the whiskey down. This is the last straw for me.

If I was mad before, I really start seeing red now. I feel blood pounding in my ears, my heart beats real fast, my mouth's dry and there's a tight pinched-up feeling between my eyes. Suddenly someone sees me standing here with the barrel of my gun resting on the floor and they all start backing away, leaving these two guys just staring at me with their arms still raised, their eyes wide and wild looking like the eyes of a cow moose in heat and their mouths gaping like big-mouthed bass. They stand there pale and frozen, like in some old-time picture. I raise my shotgun to my hip and blow a big hole clean through old Scarface's chest. His body jumps up and rips across the room and slams up against the bar before it crumples in a heap. His glass flips into the air and clatters to the floor. All the time his buddy just stands there staring, like he's paralyzed—with my thumb still floating in his drink. I blast him, too. He flies backward, tumbles over some chairs, pitches his glass right at me, and it comes crashing down at my feet.

I walk over, pick up both my thumbs out of the blood and broken glass and stuff them into the pocket of my Carhartt jacket. My thumb joints are throbbing like hell so I tell the bartender to give me a double shot. I toss it down and head on up the road looking for the other two guys.

They aren't at Rosie's, so I go on up to the Red Garter at the end of the road. It looks kind of quiet, only a few cars in the parking lot. I park my Jimmy next to a big snow bank, so it's headed back toward town.

I walk in carrying my shotgun and I look around. There're a few people I know but not the two guys I'm looking for. Everyone starts acting kind of nervous when they see me, so I suppose word of my escapade has spread ahead of me up the road. Well, I'm feeling pretty damned jittery myself by now. So I wave the shotgun around and tell everyone to lay down on the floor, which they do right away without any argument. About then, I hear the door to the men's room open up, and this young feller comes walking down the hallway back into the bar. He sees everyone laying on the floor covering up their heads and he says, "This party's getting too damn rough for me. I'm going home," and he runs for the door. I don't know why, but I raise my shotgun and pull the trigger. He screams and grabs his shoulder and starts bawling like a wounded bear. I look at this pitiful guy and realize it's Freddy, one of the kids who used to hang around our house when he and my boy, Tom, were in high school. Oh, shit! I think. What in hell have I done? Something seems to kinda snap in my brain about then and I feel sick and scared.

I go out to my pickup, thinking I probably ought to get the hell out of here and back to town. So I throw it into reverse, tromp on the gas and, don't you know, I slam right into that big snow bank, hard, and get stuck up to my axles. I try rocking it back and forth, but no luck. I'm really stuck. I get out and pull a set of chains out of the bed and try to hook one of them onto a tire, keeping the shotgun propped up right along side me there, just in case.

Then I hear sirens working their way out of town and up the Highway. I know all the cops in town—drink coffee with them every morning down at Betty's Cafe. I wonder which of 'em's on duty tonight. They probably won't want to kill me and I sure don't want to shoot any of them. They're my buddies.

I keep working with the chains, but I know it's really hopeless, what with my missing thumbs and the sirens getting closer all the time. Then they careen around the bend and their headlights come right at me. I scramble around the back of the pickup with my shotgun and drop down in the snow.

I hear them calling out for me to throw over my gun. "Come on out, Bobby," they say, so I know that they know it's me.

I start thinking about what's going to happen to me. I probably won't get much for killing those oil field scumbags but if that innocent kid dies, it'll probably go real hard on me. So I do the right thing, the only thing I can do under the circumstances. I wrap my lips over the end of the barrel, stretch hard, get a finger on the trigger, and pull.

Things go sort of wild then for a while. Everything goes dark and it feels like a whirlwind has me. Stuff flies past me. What, I can't tell for sure—maybe bird-like creatures and planets and thumbs. Thumbs? I hear weird sounds, like muffled voices far away and crying, lots of crying, women crying. I think it's gone on for an hour or two but I guess it really must have been days. Because the next thing I know things are starting to slow down and it's getting light. Finally I can see again, and I hear organ music.

I'm kind of up in a corner of what looks like the National Guard Armory building. I'm looking down at a bunch of people sitting in rows on folding chairs. I see some of my friends in the back all dude-ed up in suits and ties and looking as solemn as if someone has taken a dump in their new hats. I've never seen any of these guys in ties, so I think this must just be a dream. That is until I see them passing a flask around from one to the other, each taking a big swig every time it goes by.

Then I hear this god-awful wailing and I look toward the front of the room and there's my wife blubbering into a hankie. I'm glad to see she doesn't have that big-shot oilie guy with her. Maybe she finally came to her senses. She and my mother are sitting there with their arms wrapped around each other and carrying on something fierce. It's embarrassing. Then I see the box with the lid closed, and I know it's me in there. Kind of makes me feel strange, you know—being up here watching and being in there all at the same time.

I'm not much of one for religion, so I'm kind of

surprised when this woman I don't know, maybe the preacher's wife, gets up and sings a couple of church songs. Then the preacher gets up and starts talking about what kind of guy I was. The gist of what he says is that I've been a respectful son, okay husband, proud father, damned good worker, great friend. "But," he says, (there's always a "but" isn't there?) "If Bobby had just learned how to stay out of bars and fights this wouldn't have happened."

I want to yell down and tell him I was just a normal guy, good sometimes, and except for a bad day now and again—like last Friday night—I wasn't all that bad either. Anyway, everyone sits there nodding their heads as if they agree with everything he says. I see my dumb friends in the back wiping tears out of their eyes and whiskey off their lips. Finally the preacher says a little prayer, a nice sincere prayer really, asking for mercy for my soul. I get a little misty eyed myself I'm so touched by his concern for me.

Then everyone piles out of the building and loads into their cars. My six friends, half stewed by now, grab hold of the box and struggle with it out to the big gray hearse. "Damn, I didn't know the old sonofabitch was so heavy," one of them says. The others agree between grunts. Well, I think, a guy doesn't get to be fifty-something without putting on a few pounds.

Well, you see, the cemetery sits on a hill back off the main highway, maybe a quarter of a mile or so. The dirt road leading up to it is sticky gumbo because of the spring breakup. Wouldn't you know, the hearse gets stuck right up to its running boards, about a hundred yards off the pavement, and there it sits.

So my six tipsy pals step bravely out into that slop and grab the handles and start hauling the box up the road. Sinking in up to their ankles, they slip and slide and struggle. It isn't just the mud; it's the layer of ice under the mud meeting up with the slick soles on their dress shoes. There's loud sucking noises as their feet pull free of the muck and squishy sounds as they set them back down again. Of course, the fact that they've been nipping on that flask for God-only-knows how long doesn't seem to help their stability any. They bite their lips and mutter under their breaths as they struggle up the long sorry slope to the gravesite.

All the other mourners follow along, wading through that mess, picking their way among the tombstones. My wife, always the one to dress to the hilt for any occasion, minces along in her three-inch heels. She is still wailing, though now I suspect it's more for her ruined shoes than for me. Finally, everyone gets there, all muddy and cold, obviously hating every minute and hoping that this nightmare hurries up and gets over with.

My friends slowly start moving the casket over the hole. Suddenly the earth gives way under Moose, and he goes shooting down into that muddy pit. The weight shift happens so fast the other guys lose control of the box and it topples in right on top of him and wedges in, kind of sideways. I can just imagine my corpse bouncing around in there, those loose thumbs flying around and thumping against the lid. Well, these guys, in their new suits, climb down into the hole and pry and pull and push at that hateful box, but it's no use. All the time Moose is down there screeching and crying and pleading and begging for them to hurry up and get him out.

The mourners are standing around horrified, eyes either wide in disbelief or covered up in hopes this isn't really happening. It's the funniest damn thing I've ever seen. My wife is just bellerin' now and screaming for someone to do something and saying what a travesty this is. Good word, I think, though I'm not really sure what it means. I wonder if she does.

Finally, one of the guys decides he'd better go back to town for help. So he slogs down the hill to the cars and speeds off to town. After a painful long time, we hear a big Cat slowly working its way toward the cemetery. It comes lumbering up the road, passes the stuck hearse, and chugs up to the hole, making deep ruts across the neighboring graves. I'm thinking the families of those poor dead slobs are really going to be furious.

He hooks a chain around his bucket and heaves away at the box until it finally springs free, dangles out of the hole, and flops around like a freshly hooked salmon. Someone reaches in and gives Moose a hand up. He's pale and shaking and looks like he's just seen Jesus. "I need a drink," he says, not worried about the preacher standing there, and takes a long pull on the flask someone hands him. They pass it around to the bystanders, some of whom gladly help themselves to a snort. My wife included. She takes several big gulps, and leans heavily against a muddy, still blubbering Moose and he seems to enjoy the contact.

Then things begin to go dim and I feel myself drifting away. I guess I'm on the way to my eternal resting place. I just hope it's a long ways away from any oilie bastards. Suddenly, I see flames shooting into the sky and I smell a nasty sulphur odor. Is this hell, then, I wonder? But, no, hell's supposed to be hot. It's way too cold here—all I see is snow and more snow. Then, I understand when I see the sign—Welcome to Prudhoe Bay.

An Act of Nature

First, was the cigarette butt, a tan filter—round, clean, hard—lying on a mound of dirty snow in the alder clearing at the edge of the woods. No other sign of an intruder, just the butt.

The next morning she found her cat, its throat slit with the precision of a surgeon. The ribbed trachea flopped nakedly from the wound, still oozing blood onto her porch.

A few days later, the footprint. Just one, a thick diamond-within-diamond pattern; a square heel—like a man's hiking boot—pressed deeply into the soft soil of the path where it crossed the creek.

After finding the owl the following morning—hanging from a hemp rope in the lilac bush blooming by the back door, both amber eyes gouged out of its puffy, misshapen head—she decided it was time to report these strange incidences to the police.

"You're living in the old Miller place, aren't you, way out at the end of Deadman's Road?" the sheriff asked. "Folks talk like it's a spooky place, with them strange goin's on out there now and again. Some of them stories got you a bit paranoid? Well you needn't worry, all of 'em been explained—generally just one strange act of nature or another. Ain't that right, Ernie?"

Ernie, the fat deputy, sat ogling Deirdre, his feet propped on his desk. "Yes, ma'am," he said. "Living alone can do strange things to a person. You do live alone, don't you, Miss Lang?" The way his eyes swept up and down her athletic frame made her skin crawl.

"Maybe you're right," she said, looking back at the sheriff, preferring to ignore the deputy's lewdness. "But, I don't exactly call mutilated animals 'natural occurrences,' do you?"

"I'd be looking at one of your students, some kid with a grudge over a failing grade, trying to get even," the sheriff said.

"Maybe," she said. "But I don't like having someone creeping around out there in the woods, especially since the only way into it is from my backyard."

"Well, I recollect there's an old jeep road up on the ridge behind there. Remember that road, Ernie?"

The deputy rubbed a beefy hand over the dark stubble on his chin, rolled his eyes toward the ceiling as if trying to recall, then said, "Yeah, I do sorta remember it. Maybe whoever it is comes in from there." Both men laughed as if at some private joke.

"Well, I'll bet if you take some time to think about it and check it out, you'll probably find some biology freshman with a bad attitude."

She saw it was useless to expect help from this quarter and turned to leave.

"Let us know if we can be of further help, you hear?" The deputy grinned and, with a fingernail, picked at something between his yellowed teeth. He winked wickedly at Deirdre.

Disgusted, she left without looking back.

When she received a hateful note on final exam papers from a disgruntled student, she began to think the sheriff might have been correct in his analysis. Nevertheless, she stopped going into the woods and stayed close to the house, keeping doors and windows locked until after the spring semester was over. The following Saturday she adopted a three-year-old Husky from the animal shelter—just for companionship, she told herself.

One day a couple of months later, in mid-July, Deirdre sat reading in a lounge chair on her back porch, King asleep at her feet. Suddenly a flicker of light glinting from the alders caught her attention—just a flash, then gone—gone so fast it might have been her imagination. But one look at the dog—now on his feet staring in the same direction, ears pricked, the hair along his neck stiff and erect—told her something, or someone, was out there.

Her anger flared. She stood, threw down her book, and strode towards the gate. "King, come," she demanded. He was already ahead of her, bounding across the yard, disappearing into the trees. She ran after him, adrenaline pushing her forward, until she caught sight of the dog ahead on the trail, hackles raised, a deep throaty growl reaching her ears as she approached him. She heard the sounds of snapping twigs as someone or something ran away.

She stopped, her initial rush of anger subsiding into caution. Deirdre stood riveted to the spot where she'd found the cigarette butt in early spring.

"Probably just a moose," she heard her own shaking voice assuring the dog. "Want to have a look?" she asked, moving past him. They stepped slowly through the trees, Deirdre searching and King sniffing for signs. Then she saw a tiny shred of fabric dangling from the end of a branch. It was green camouflage, like hunters wear, torn and fluttering from a protruding snag. Beneath the tree, diamond-within-diamond boot print patterns, like the other.

She spent the rest of the day behind locked doors and windows, peering out frequently towards the clearing.

When King didn't return from his bedtime run that evening, even after urgent, repeated calls, Deirdre was too nervous to sleep. She sat up the rest of the night, gripped with fear, staring from the darkness of her room into blackness outside.

At first light, equipped with a butcher knife concealed under her jacket—the only thing she owned that resembled a weapon—she slipped out a little-used side door, which was partially obscured from view by overgrown bushes. She dashed across an open space to a row of sheds, slipped behind them, and then stood at the corner several minutes, searching the trees for any movement. Finally, she plunged across another unprotected space to reach the cover of the trees. Light had not yet penetrated into the forest as she moved cautiously forward trying to avoid making noise. She glanced nervously to the sides and behind, alert for any movement or sound. At last she neared the spot where she'd found the torn fabric. She stood still several minutes, scarcely daring to breath, listening and looking. Satisfied at last that she was alone, she ventured ahead, passed the tree with the snag, and found fresh dog tracks. At first she supposed they were from the day before, then she realized they continued on, following a game trail deeper into the woods.

She tensed, her pulse quickened, and she touched the knife under her jacket, debating whether to draw it into the open. She pulled it out. Then, feeling foolish, she concealed it again.

"This is stupid," she told herself. "The dog probably got into a pack of coyotes or followed a stray bitch in heat. And some careless hunter undoubtedly tore that piece of cloth last fall. Get a grip!"

She felt better—more like her sensible, practical self— and stepped more boldly ahead on the path. She hadn't felt truly secure since her divorce. But she was working through it—had her job, her students, her dog. Yet, the thought of King missing all night brought another wave of fear.

"What about that flash of light and the boot prints?" she asked herself. "Explain them." She couldn't. Now, without hesitation, she again pulled the knife from her jacket, grasped it like a dagger, and crept along the trail. She rounded a huge boulder and stopped in her tracks. What she saw made her gasp. A dark, hairy form, nearly hidden from view in a thicket of bushes, lay just off the trail.

She heard a shriek—hideous, unearthly, not seeming to belong to her—ricochet through the forest, bouncing from tree to tree like a living demon. Then, silence. Reverberating, oppressive silence.

The dog's glassy eyes of death stared at her. He had strangled in a coyote snare. Dropping the knife, she stumbled backward, her hand over her mouth, attempting to hold down the bile that rose in her throat. Then she turned and ran, stumbling along the trail, unmindful of everything except of the need to get away. She was unaware of tears streaming down her face, or the man approaching through the trees, until she ran blindly into him. She screamed again.

Ernie, the deputy, breathing hard from exertion, grabbed her. She tried to free herself from his grip, twisting and kicking.

"Sonofabitch!" he yelled, when her teeth sank into his forearm. "Hold on, you little hellcat! What's got you so riled up, anyway?"

Not recognizing him and blind with fear, she continued to struggle. "Let me go," she yelled.

"Sure, but only when you tell me what's going on. I was in the area and thought I'd stop by and check on you. You didn't answer your door. When I saw your back gate open, I got kinda worried and started lookin' for you," he said. He'd loosened his grip on her arm and she finally stopped struggling. "I was just in that clearing over there and I came as fast as I could when I heard you scream."

Her relief briefly overcame her mistrust of him, and she led him back to where the dog lay. She was relieved to see her butcher knife had fallen into the bushes, out of sight.

"I'll be damned," he said, almost reverently. "I hain't seen a coyote snare in years."

"Someone's after me," she sobbed. "There is someone

stalking me, someone who keeps watching my house."

"Nah, I doubt that. Just another of them things that seems eerie, but that's probably easy to explain. Bet this snare's been here forever, probably set by old Mr. Miller himself, ages ago when he trapped these here woods. You gotta stop being so paranoid."

He walked her back to the house. "I'm sure sorry about the dog. I'll have someone come out and fetch him for you," he said as he left.

She watched from the window as Ernie checked his reflection in the rearview mirror, running a comb through his unruly hair before getting out of the car and coming back to the door. He made her uneasy and she wished he would leave.

"If you don't mind, I'll drop by later. You know, just to be sure you're okay."

She was repulsed by the thought. "Don't bother, please. I think I'll be going to bed early tonight."

When he was gone, she showered, changed clothes, and then drove to town. She did not stop at the sheriff's office but went instead to see Matt, one of her ex-husband's friends. She hadn't seen him, or Sally, his wife, since her divorce. But Matt had always been nice to her and she knew he would be willing to loan her what she'd come for.

"Hello, Matt," she said to the pair of legs protruding from under a station wagon. He slid out from under the vehicle, wiping grease from his hands, and led her to the house.

"You sure you know how to use this thing?" he asked, as he handed her the "Cobra," a .38 caliber snub-nosed pistol.

"Don't you remember Danny's insistence that I learn,

even though I hated the things?" she asked. "All those Saturday trips to the rifle range?"

"Oh, yeah, I remember," he said. "Coyotes, you say? Well, this little baby should do the trick. Keep it as long as you need."

"Thanks. I'll get it back to you soon," she said as he walked her back to her car. She waved and watched him disappear again under the station wagon.

She made one more stop, this time at the dry goods store, to buy a pair of binoculars. Then she drove toward home. A wave of sadness washed over her as she met and passed an animal control pickup coming from her place and knew King had been disposed of.

Later, sitting with a good view of the woods from behind drawn blinds and in a darkened house, she trained her new binoculars on them, watching and waiting, through the long afternoon hours. Finally, just before ten o'clock, as the long daylight hours hinted at dusk, she caught movement. A figure, dressed in green camouflage, stepped from the trees at the edge of the clearing. She could not make out the features of the man, but saw he was large—not fat, but muscular, tall, shoulders slightly stooped, head jutted forward as if probing his way. He wore a hat drawn close over his face, dark glasses hiding his eyes. For several minutes he stood puffing on a cigarette—drawing in long draughts, exhaling streams of smoke—and looking towards her house. She held her breath and did not move for fear he might somehow sense her presence behind the blinds.

The man finished smoking, stubbed the cigarette out, put the butt in a pocket, and walked a few steps to a clump of bushes. She watched as he knelt, reached far back under them and pulled something out. He stood again, moved a few feet back into the trees, and took up a position on a fallen log. She saw the glint of the dying sun reflect off binocular glass and knew a pair of evil eyes was watching her house. A chill slid along her shoulders, up her neck and across her cheeks, making the fine hairs prickle.

She continued to watch the watcher. Just before dark, he rose from his secluded spot, returned the field glasses to the bushes, and disappeared into the forest.

The two lawmen were condescending again when she reported the latest incident to them. "Now I ain't calling you a liar, but this here's a free country and if there was a man in the woods he's got as much right to be there as you do. You don't own them woods, you know." The sheriff sounded edgy and impatient. "You city women—no offense—just think all men are no good. This here's the safest place in the world. Ain't that right?" He sighed heavily, shrugged and looked at Ernie, who watched from his desk—feet crossed, as usual, on top of it.

"That's just what I told he, myself." The fat deputy slowly removed first one foot then the other from the desktop. He sauntered over and leaned across the counter, putting his oily face close to hers. "I even offered to drop by and keep her company, but she didn't act like she was interested in companionship," he said sarcastically.

Deirdre backed away, repulsed by both the slaver on his meaty lips and the garlic on his breath. Giving them each a long, thoughtful look, but not saying another word, she left, thoroughly discouraged and disgusted.

Later that week she bought a nearly grown puppy—a registered, thick-chested, black and gray malamute—and christened him Ringo. She was determined to never let him out of her sight.

During the rest of the summer—in between working on lesson plans for the fall semester, gardening, and numerous science projects—watching the woods became her daily habit. She tried to chart the intruder's routine, but after a month, found it so sporadic it was impossible. He might show up several days in a row, then not be seen for more than a week. Sometimes he was there for hours, other times for just a few minutes. The only consistent thing she found was that it was always later in the day when he came.

She kept Ringo close by, always going out with him for runs, never leaving his side for even a moment. She left him shut in the house that morning in late August when she gathered the courage to go to the stalker's spot, her curiosity overcoming her fear. She searched for his cache in the bushes and found it, well hidden under the thick overhanging branches—a five-gallon bucket buried in the ground. In it were a pair of leather gloves, the binoculars, a sharp skinning knife, a lighter, an unopened pack of Winston cigarettes, a pair of wool socks and a small leather pouch containing several Polaroid snapshots of various bloody, mangled animals—the cat and owl among them. The horror of it all nauseated and disgusted her. She quickly threw everything back into the cache, then thinking better, she emptied them out again and carefully replaced all the items in the order she'd found them.

Moments later she left, sweeping the area with a green branch to erase her footprints, and followed the path he apparently used to its source, staying just off the edge so as to leave no obvious prints. The trail climbed to the top of a ridge, terminating at last on a deeply rutted and overgrown roadway—the one the sheriff had mentioned that first time she went to his office. Numerous tire tracks in a flat grassy area a few feet away, where the weeds were matted down, showed where he'd parked a vehicle. She walked half a mile back along the road, looking for and finding a different route back towards her house. Stopping to rest, she realized that where she now sat was above the clearing the man frequented, and that from here she could easily see down into it without him knowing she was here, giving her a slight advantage.

One morning a few days later, when she let him out, Ringo seemed curious and fascinated by something in a pot of red geraniums growing on the porch. She heard the fatal warning buzz of the rattler the same instant the pup yelped. Before she could reach him, he was twitching in convulsions on the floor, froth bubbling from his mouth. Moments later he lay dead.

Fury, not despair, overtook her, propelling her into action. "I will not allow that vile stalker to harm even one more poor innocent animal," she screamed. "Never again!"

Running to the shed, she grabbed a hoe and sped back in time to see the snake slither from the flowerpot. She pressed its murderous head to the floor. With shaking hands she grasped it at the base of its head, as she had seen snake handlers do, and deposited the writhing viper into an empty Styrofoam ice chest stored on the porch.

She emerged from the house a short time later wearing hiking gear and a backpack. In it were her binoculars, a thermos of coffee, a jacket, and the pistol. As she picked up the ice chest, the startled snake began to rattle, the sound electric and hollow.

When she'd finished her task in the clearing the man frequented, Deirdre climbed up to that spot she'd found on her investigative trip a few days before—the one near the back road where she'd discovered that she could watch him, undetected.

She sat on her rock, waiting, and as time slowly dragged by she began to worry. What if he didn't come today?

But around four o'clock, she heard a vehicle whining along the old road. It lumbered past, slowed, stopped. She listened to the door open, close. No further sound. She waited fifteen minutes—long enough, she thought, for him to arrive in the clearing—then she really started to worry when he didn't appear as soon as she thought he should. Maybe he's on to me, she thought, knows I've discovered his stash. Her muscles ached from tension, from sitting still so long. But she dared not move any more than to make slight adjustments so she could see better.

At last, relieved, she saw him. He stepped into the clearing in his stealthy way, studying the house while he pulled a cigarette from his pocket and smoked. As was his habit, when he'd finished smoking he stubbed it out and put the butt in his pocket. She watched him through her binoculars as he went to his bucket hidden in the bushes.

When she thought about it later, she remembered it all in slow motion. He was kneeling, then leaning over the spot where the bucket was concealed, then his right arm was extending slowly out and down, then retracting back and up, shaking what appeared to be a thick, diamond-patterned rope attached to his forearm. Then he was stumbling to his feet, staggering in a circle, grasping the object with his free hand, as if trying to fling the thing off. He finally freed himself of it, then he lurched—like a very slow robot, it seemed to her—out of sight into the trees.

The next morning she was calm and not in the least surprised when the sheriff and his deputy appeared at her door. She'd heard their vehicle hours earlier and had watched them driving slowly back and forth along the road. She'd seen them as they tramped around in the woods.

"Come in. Coffee?" She felt almost light-hearted and happy, bolstered by the first full night's sleep she'd had in months.

"We came to talk to you about Pete," the sheriff said as soon as they were seated at the kitchen table.

Deirdre calmly poured coffee into two mugs. "Pete? I don't know anyone by that name," she said. "Cream or sugar?"

"I think you do." Ernie's voice cracked. His obvious agitation made his eyes bulge from his pudgy red face. "He's—er, that is he was—my pappy's cousin. Lived alone in a cabin up on top the mountain, there." The deputy's flaccid lips quivered and it looked as if he might cry, even as he indicated that he wanted both sugar and cream.

"Sorry, don't think I ever met the man," Deirdre said.

"All them weird things you had happening, well, we suspected it might have something to do with him," the sheriff said. "He's always been a little 'off'—if you know what I mean, but he was harmless. Absolutely harmless. We didn't worry none. We just figured he liked sneaking down here to get a look at a pretty woman, and there's no law against anyone just looking. He'd never have hurt you."

"That's exactly what he said, too," Ernie chimed in, "after we went to talk to him, you know, the first time you came in to the office."

"What about the animal mutilations?" she asked icily. "There's no excuse for what he did to them!"

"I couldn't figure out about the animals either, and he wouldn't say," the sheriff said. "Finally we figured out he was probably just jealous of them getting your attention, wishing it was him instead."

"That's sick! Horrible!" she screamed, suddenly in a rage. "There's no excuse for the terrible things he did to those poor creatures!"

"We did feel real bad about the animals," the sheriff said, trying to make his voice sound soothing. "Especially the dogs."

"He should be severely punished!" She fled to the cool of the back porch, trying to quiet her shaking and regain some composure.

"Oh, I think he's been punished very severely." The sheriff had followed her outside. "He turned up dead this morning. Dead, not over five hundred yards from here, right there in your woods," he said.

"Oh, dear," she heard herself say, surprised at the sudden return of steadiness in her voice. Perhaps her small bit of theatrical training was paying off. "In my woods? What happened? Did he have a heart attack, or something?"

"No. He got himself bit by a rattler. Right over there." He pointed to the clearing now so familiar to her.

"A rattler? That's strange. Rattlesnakes don't live in Alaska," she said.

"I know that," the sheriff said, studying her face. "I figured you, being a biology teacher, you'd know all about that, too."

She shrugged. "Sometimes, as you say, there's just no explanation for the strange acts of nature, is there?" she said, looking him steadily in the eye.

Fire & Brimstone

Junior and Royal stood mid-block in front of Old Red, Junior's one-ton Dodge flatbed truck, each with a heel hooked on the front bumper. It was Friday, and they were waiting for their friend, Dale—the only one of the three who had any kind of regular income—to cash his paycheck at the bank located at the end of the street. Dale had promised to buy a case of beer. Then they were going out to the gravel pit to sight-in their rifles. Hunting season was just around the corner, and they wanted to be ready.

Junior, his short-sleeved shirt unbuttoned to his navel and with a cheek full of chew, spit a stream into the street. A gold nugget, dangling from a heavy chain, glistened from amongst the gray-black hair of his chest. He absentmindedly twisted the nugget between thick, rough fingers, anxious to get going. He was starting to get fidgety, wondering 'what the gol-dang' was keeping Dale in the bank so long.

Royal vigorously puffed on an unfiltered Camel, blowing smoke rings into the air. His close-set eyes squinted

impatiently in the direction of the bank. Just then, the bank
door opened and Mrs. Pruitt came out.

"Hey," Royal said, "ain't that Old Lady Pruitt—the
Bible banger?"

"Yeah, that's her," said Junior.

"Ain't she the one that's always on you to give up your
sinning and start going to church?" Royal asked.

"Yeah, that's her," Junior said. "She can be a giant
pain in the ass, nosing into my business like she does
sometimes."

At that precise moment, two boys raced along the
street chasing a little dog. They nearly collided with the
woman, and as the two men watched, Mrs. Pruitt reached out
faster than a frog's tongue catching a fly and snatched one of
the boys by an arm. She shook her finger under his nose,
obviously giving him a lecture. The other boy escaped around
the corner of the bank and peeked back to watch his friend's
distress.

"Hey, I got 'n idea! Wanna have a little fun?" Junior
asked.

"Sure," Royal said.

"Get in." The two of them jumped in Old Red and
Junior started up the engine. He eased carefully up to Mrs.
Pruitt's car—luckily parked right in front of his truck—and
pushed his iron grill up against the rear bumper of her big
maroon Caddy.

"Oh, she'll just shit," said Royal.

"Yeah," Junior grinned. "Ain't it gonna be great?"

They watched her start down the street. She had a
way of standing out in a crowd—her hair all twisted up in that

tight little bun, black dress buttoned clear to her chin, ugly cotton hose, and silly high heels that made her walk like an amateur aerialist on a tightrope. And she always had that worn-out old Bible shoved into her armpit as if it grew there.

She bustled on down the street. As she drew closer, a woman and her young son stepped out of another store. Mrs. Pruitt stopped short and bent to fuss over the little guy. The two men in the truck overheard her crooning, "My, my, Tommy, aren't you the sweetest little man?" She patted the disgusted-looking child on the cheek. "One of God's precious little angels," she said to the mother as she tickled him under the chin. She straightened up and looked accusingly in the young woman's face.

"Mary, I don't remember seeing you in church last Sunday," she scolded. "I surely do hope you have a good excuse. This youngster needs Sunday school. You know what the Bible says about bringing up a child in the way he should go, so he'll not depart from it!"

The mother, obviously embarrassed, mumbled something, pulled the child by his arm and began walking away. "I'll be praying for you," Mrs. Pruitt shouted after the retreating pair.

Junior reached across the seat and tapped Royal on the arm. "See, that's just the way she talks to me," he said.

She continued on down the street toward the two men sitting in Old Red. As she came near her car, she stopped again, this time to talk with a young man just coming from the hardware store.

"Hello, Mrs. Pruitt. How are you this fine morning?" he asked, respectfully removing his hat.

"I'm just peachy keen, Brother Brown," she said. "It's so good to see you're out doing the Lord's work this beautiful day." They chatted a few moments, and then Junior and Royal heard her say, "You know, Preacher, I've been meaning to talk to you. It seems to me that your sermons just haven't quite been up to par of late. They've been lacking drive, if you know what I mean, getting a little lukewarm for my tastes, and you remember what God said about 'lukewarm'—how those who are neither hot nor cold, He will spew out of His mouth. I think some of the people in this church, and this community," she flung her free arm wide to take in the whole town, including the men sitting in the truck, "could use some shaking up. I know you're still young and I don't expect you to be able to fill the shoes of Brother Thomas—bless his dear departed soul—but you should try harder."

The man couldn't get in a word edgewise and just stood nodding—meekly, it seemed to the watching pair.

"I'm telling you," Mrs. Pruitt continued, "We need us a good revival in this town, that's a fact. The sinning that's going on is just shocking."

"Poor bastard," Junior said, shaking his head empathetically.

"Yes, ma'am, I suppose you are right. I am trying my best," the young preacher stammered, his face flushed. He hastily replaced his hat, muttered something about having to rush—the annual board meeting at the church was discussing whether to renew his call for another year. He hurried away.

"I'll be praying for you, Brother Brown," she shouted after him.

At last she turned toward her car. At first she didn't

see that Junior had her blocked in. She went around the front, opened the door, tossed her purse and Bible across the seat, then climbed in. The two men watched her pull on driving gloves, start the engine, put the car into reverse, and twist around to look behind her before backing out of her parking space. She just sat there as if she couldn't quite make out what she saw out her back window.

Then she jerked around, swung open her door, jumped out and started marching back to Junior's truck.

When they saw her heading their direction, Junior and Royal hurriedly rolled up the windows and pretended to be engrossed in something happening on the sidewalk. She rapped on the window. Then thumped harder. Junior slowly looked around in feigned surprise and cranked the window down a bit. "Howdy, Mrs. Pruitt. How are you?"

She didn't answer. Her face was turning red, and her snapping black eyes looked like they might pop out of her head.

"Is something wrong?" he asked innocently.

"You!...You!...You!" She bit the word off crisply each time she said it, as if she were snapping green beans. "Junior Deville, you know very well what is wrong," she finally spit out. "You are parked up against my car so I can't get out!"

"Oh, so I am," he said. "Yep, guess that's true." He didn't move.

"Well?" She tapped a foot impatiently. "Well?" When he didn't respond she shouted, "Move it!"

"Oh, I'm not ready to go yet. I'm waiting for my friend. I don't see him coming, do you?" he asked Royal. They both stared up the street, pretending to ignore the irritated woman.

"I said move it," she screeched from behind clenched teeth. "I have things to do. Move it now—or else."

"Or else?" He asked. "Or else, what, Mrs. Pruitt?"

"I'll call Sheriff Ron, and he'll make you move," she yelled, raising a fist as if to strike him. The tattooed serpent on his arm appeared to be uncoiling when he flexed the muscles, moving his arm as if to deflect her blow. She lowered her hand. Turning on her heel, she flounced back toward her car. On the way, she stopped, hauled off, and swiftly kicked the front tire of Old Red. Her face was crimson. She jabbed at the tire again, so ferociously that the heel snapped off her shoe. She hip-hopped stormily back to her car, got in, and slammed the door so hard it rocked the two men who sat grinning in the truck.

Junior and Royal looked at each other and roared with laughter. "Ain't you gonna let her out really?" Royal asked.

"Naw, let her sweat."

A few moments later Dale finally strolled out of the bank. Royal slid to the middle and Dale got in. Junior started the engine, backed up, and pulled around the fuming Mrs. Pruitt. She shook her fist at them as they passed.

They stopped at the liquor store to get the case of beer Dale promised, then headed on out to the gravel pit to start target practicing. They sighted-in all of their hunting rifles, then plunked away with their pistols at empty beer bottles tossed into the air like skeet. Betting on who was the fastest, they tried quick draws, missing most of the time, but when one of them did hit a bottle he cackled gleefully and strutted around for the benefit of the other two. But after an hour or so, they got bored.

There was still half a case of beer left when Royal got his bright idea. He'd heard of a powder man working on the North Slope who'd astounded everyone by using a dynamite charge to move an entire mountain of gravel across a railroad track, saving the company the time and effort of moving it all with loaders and trucks. Well, his pal, Junior, here, was about as good a powder man as could be found. So, reminding Junior and Dale of the incident, Royal threw down the challenge.

"Hey, Junior, lookie there. See that pile of gravel? What'd you bet you could send it sailing over that railroad car without damaging anything?"

Junior's face lit up. "Piece a cake," he said. "All I need is a little dynamite. And, just guess what's in that railcar that says "Property of Alyeska Pipeline" on it? See, even painted in big bold letters: EXPLOSIVES, KEEP OUT. I doubt they'll mind if we borrow a few sticks."

Junior had worked off and on for Alyeska and had, in fact, just been laid off two weeks ago, and he knew the combination to the lock. The three of them set about the task of moving boxes of dynamite to the gravel pile. Then, giving precise instructions to his two helpers, Junior meticulously set the charge.

He was just about to push the plunger, when Royal said, "Wait! Why don't we go round up a bunch of the boys at Shorty's Bar and make a bet on this deal?"

"Great idea," Dale chimed in. So, Royal and Dale jumped in Old Red and sped off to town. Within thirty minutes a parade of pickups careened down the gravel pit road, throwing plumes of dust into the air. They all screeched to a stop; vehicle doors flew open and men poured out, all talking at once.

"Shorty's holding a pot of twelve hundred bucks," Royal whispered to Junior. "Fifty bucks a pop to get in on the deal." He wiggled his eyebrows up and down, obviously pleased at his own genius.

Dale stood nervously rubbing the side of his face, looking worried. "What if we lose the bet?" he said.

"Aw, hell, quit your worrying. You know Junior's the best powder man in the state. Probably in the whole United States of America for that matter," Royal said. "Relax and think about how we're going to spend our winnings."

Junior held up his hand for silence. "Okay, boys," he said, strumming his thick fingers, fanfare fashion, on his hairy chest as if it were a drum. "This gravel pile will move from here, over that railroad car, and down the other side without spilling on the car."

His pronouncement was met with jeers and laughs. The rowdy bunch of spectators clanked beer bottles together and made gestures of rubbing fifty dollar bills between fingers and thumbs. Junior, stroking the gold nugget dangling on his chest, walked ceremoniously over to the plunger. The crowd disappeared behind their pickups.

"What a bunch of sissy-asses," Junior taunted. "Come on, you gutless bastards. Stand here beside me." He pushed down on the plunger. He didn't move—just stood there, lightly covering his ears. There was dead silence. Everyone held his breath. Then, as if on cue, in whispered unison, they started counting. Ten, nine, eight, seven, six, five, four, three, two, one. Kaboom!!! And then, just milliseconds later, there was a second blast.

It was as if the mound of gravel had been sitting on a magic carpet. It rose into the air, seemingly hovered a moment, floated across the railroad car and settled down in almost exactly the same shape on the other side. Mouths dropped open. The silence was thick enough to wring out like a wet towel. They all gazed at Junior—this man they called "crazy barbarian"—with looks of new respect. They'd just witnessed the impossible.

"I'm good," he said without a shred of humility or embarrassment, as if trying to explain it. "Damned good."

The next morning, Junior slept in. Loud pounding on the door of his Airstream trailer interrupted his dreams. He dragged himself out of bed, pulled on dirty jeans, hoisted suspenders over his hairy barrel chest, and peered out. There stood Sheriff Ron.

"Morning, Junior. Mrs. Pruitt paid me a call yesterday, filing a complaint against you. Said you were causing trouble again," he said.

"Aw, hell, Sheriff, I was just having a little fun with the old bat. She just ain't never learned to take a joke," Junior sputtered.

"Well, I promised her I'd come out here and talk to you, and I guess I've done that. Have a nice day, Junior. See you around."

Now that he was awake, Junior finished dressing and went to town. He walked into Betty's Cafe, settled himself at the counter, and ordered a cup of strong coffee. He noticed the young minister sitting alone in a corner booth.

The preacher slowly left his seat, walked up to Junior

and held out his hand. "Mr. Deville," he said. "I'm Reverend Brown, the new minister."

Junior looked at the man without interest. "Yes sir. I know who you are," he said, not offering his hand in return.

The preacher stood awkwardly with his outstretched palm, then pulled it back and nervously stuck it in his pocket. He cleared his throat and looked away from Junior's poker face, then, as if with great determination, he faced him again. "I don't know how to say this exactly," he said, "but a lady in my congregation—Mrs. Esther Pruitt, I suppose you know her—has asked me to speak to you. She's concerned about you, seems to think you may have some problems that you could use help with. I just want you to know that I am here to help if I can," he concluded lamely.

Junior looked at the man blankly. "Thank you, sir. But, really, I'm doin' just fine. I doubt I'll be needin' your help. I'll sure keep you in mind if ever I do though." With that, Junior turned away and poured sugar into his coffee, ignoring the other man.

Apparently not entirely daunted by Junior's rude behavior he said, "I'd just like to extend an invitation for you to join us for church tomorrow. You would be very welcome, I'm sure."

Junior grunted and shrugged. He was having a hard time keeping his thoughts to himself. The encounters with the sheriff and now the preacher were starting to really rankle him. He didn't much care for it—having that old bat turn him in to the law and now to God as well. He shoved his coffee cup away and stood abruptly, nearly knocking the other man over.

About eight o'clock the next morning—early for Junior on a Sunday morning—he rallied Royal and Dale. "Come on, you guys, we're going to church," he said. "We have a mission to fulfill."

"What?" Royal shouted.

"Have you lost your mind?" Dale yelled.

"I had me a vision," was all Junior would say as he herded them into Old Red. Before church even started, their careful preparations had been made. They perched on a mound of boulders in Mr. Wheeler's field behind the little white church, looking like three conniving crows on a fence.

It was one of those rare sunny mornings, hot, as a matter of fact, by Alaska standards—up in the seventies. All the windows in the church were open. Junior, Royal, and Dale sat on that pile of rocks, smoking and chewing, listening to the sounds coming from the church. They heard the choir singing, which sounded pretty good, except for every once in awhile when Mrs. Pruitt's voice screeched above the rest. They cringed when that happened—it hurt their ears that bad. Then everything got quiet so they figured the folks were praying. Then more singing—the whole congregation now—*Rock of Ages, cleft for me, let me hide myself in Thee.*

Then they could hear the preacher start his sermon, at first in just a kind of droning, monotone voice, and they couldn't make out the words. Gradually the volume increased a little; the pitch and tenor became clearer. Pretty soon they heard other voices in the church offering amens and hallelujahs of encouragement. The preacher's voice continued to grow louder, with greater emphasis on words like "repent " and "heaven" and "eternal damnation." To the three men sitting on the rock pile in Mr. Wheeler's field, it sounded like the preacher had taken to heart his admonishment from Mrs. Pruitt and was giving it his all. The powerful sermon wafted across the airwaves. Mrs. Pruitt's squawking "amens," charged with fire and enthusiasm and sharp as flint, stood out from the other voices.

The preacher was obviously reaching the climax of his sermon, his voice feverish, impassioned, almost that of a trained actor, as if he knew he was experiencing the greatest success of his young career right here, right now, this very Sunday morning. Every word was uttered so dramatically the three men could imagine spittle flying from his lips as he cried, "It is time to repent from your wicked ways. King David warned us..."

Junior knew the moment for fulfilling his vision and completing the mission was getting close. The timing had to be perfect, but then, Junior was a master of timing. The three men moved off their rocky perch. Junior spit a stream of chew onto the ground, wiped his hands on his pants and then hit the plunger. Ten seconds, counting down.

The preacher's voice continued, "....in Psalms 11:6, *upon the wicked he shall rain snares, fire and brimstone.*"

At that precise moment the pile of rocks exploded into a zillion pieces, jettisoned across the field, and rained down all over the roof of that little white church. Junior and the boys were already in Old Red speeding away.

When Sheriff Ron drove up to the gravel pit an hour later, the three didn't see him at first. They were holding a rambunctious private celebration. Between gulps from their beer bottles and shooting pistols into the air, they each took turns pretending to be the preacher, Mrs. Pruitt, or some other member of the congregation, acting out the various imagined scenarios of what happened as the rocks hit the church.

Royal was staggering around, one hand grasping his chest, the other hand flailing wildly, shouting, "It's my heart. I'm coming, Jesus."

Dale was crumpled over on his knees, pretending to be loudly praying for forgiveness of his many sins, listing them in their more vulgar versions.

And Junior stood on the front bumper of Old Red, facing the other two, his highway map raised over his head using it as a Bible and yelling, "I told you sinner bastards you'd die if you didn't quit screwing up!"

"Good afternoon, gentlemen," Sheriff Ron said.

The three men jumped like they'd been shot. "Howdy, Ron," Junior said. They suddenly dropped the play-acting and gathered around the sheriff.

"Well, boys." There was a long pause while the sheriff struggled to suppress a grin. "It looks like you really did it this time, Junior Deville. I think I'm going to have to haul you all in on this one."

"I suppose so," Junior said. "But this weren't Royal and Dale's doin'. Was all my own idea. They just did what I told 'em to do."

"Doesn't matter," the sheriff said. "I got to take you all in. You can explain it to the judge."

"Aw, shit," Junior sputtered. "Well, you don't need them gol-dang cuffs. We'll come along quietly."

"I know. Go ahead and drive your truck home, Junior. I'll follow you and pick you up there. You other two come with me." They went obediently.

The next two days, they wiled away the time in a joint cell, playing checkers and poker.

On Wednesday morning, the judge, who was fortunately a member of the other church in town, set bail at five thousand dollars each. About two o'clock Sheriff Ron came back to their cells and said, "All right, boys. I guess you're free to go."

"Really? Who went our bail?" Junior asked, perplexed. "I've called every one of my sonsabitchin' so-called friends and none of 'em would even talk to me. Same with Royal and Dale. And you can bet none of em's ever goin' get any favors from me, not even a nickel beer at Shorty's! So, who was it?"

"The Reverend."

"Preacher Brown?"

"Yep. He's in the interrogation room. Wants to have a word with you," the sheriff said, as he shook their personal belongings out of a manila envelope. Royal and Dale glanced at Junior ruefully, gathered up their things, and walked outside to wait for him.

Through the window to the small room Junior saw the young preacher seated at a table, clasping and unclasping his hands. He looked up when Junior walked in, smiled nervously, stood and extended a hand. Junior saw the pastor wince with pain at his vigorous grip.

"I don't know why you did it, " Junior said, playing with the gold nugget, cradled once again in the curly hair on his chest, "but I sure as hell wanna thank you for goin' our bail."

"It's all my pleasure," the preacher beamed, pretending not to notice Junior's choice of words. After a pause, he cleared this throat in that nervous way of his and said, "It was the most incredible thing. I've been trying to find a way to reach this congregation—to get them to accept me as their pastor—and more importantly to bring them closer to God. It's been very discouraging. This past week was particularly so."

Junior knew he was referring to the public reaming out he'd received from Old Lady Pruitt the other day. At the time he'd kind of felt sorry for him—almost a kinship to another man who'd been a victim of Mrs. Pruitt's sharp tongue—even though he never would have admitted it to anyone.

"So I've been praying for a sign," Reverend Brown continued softly, "to show me if I should give up and go back home to Minnesota or stick it out here."

Junior had heard the talk of the town—knew that at the church board meeting the vote for keeping the minister had been a split. He watched the preacher fiddle with his hands, seemingly lost in thought.

Then with a light in his eye, the young man straightened his shoulders and continued. "When I started to preach on Sunday, I felt the power of the Lord come upon me in a mighty way all through the service. And then I could hardly believe it myself, Brother Deville, the timing was that perfect." He became more animated as he spoke. "It was while I was reading the scripture about God raining fire and brimstone on the wicked that those rocks started pounding all over the roof of the church."

Junior openly grinned. He was touched by the preacher's enthusiasm.

"Well, when the clatter stopped, why, you could have heard a pin drop. Every eye was wide with fear. Even dear Mrs. Pruitt was clasping her hands over her heart." The preacher chuckled. Junior laughed too, remembering how funny Royal had been acting out that scene at the gravel pit.

Gathering his composure the pastor continued. "I immediately saw the hand of God at work, and I gave an invitation for sinners to come forward. The altar was filled with repentant sinners even before the first stanza of Amazing Grace was finished. Such a prayer meeting," he wagged his head in wonder. "I wouldn't have believed it possible in this town if I hadn't seen it with my own eyes. And, when it was all over, I passed the collection plate and it came back full and overflowing."

Junior didn't know what to say, so just sat watching emotions play across the younger man's face. It was flushed with excitement, commitment, satisfaction.

"Yes sir, my dear Brother Deville, as the scripture says, the Lord surely works in mysterious ways His wonders to perform. Who'd ever guess He'd be able to use such a..." Here he faltered, seeming to search for a word that would not be too insulting. "...A non-church going man, like yourself, to bring the sheep back into the fold?"

"Well, that's good, I guess, Preacher?" Junior said. "But that still don't tell me why you put up bail for me and my friends. So what's the catch?"

"Yes, well, there is one condition to your bail."

"Oh, no!" Junior said, all the while thinking, well,

here it comes!

"The committee has decided that you and your friends will be responsible for doing all of the repairs to the church," the preacher said.

Junior audibly sighed in relief, surprised that the condition was so simple.

Then the preacher continued, a mischievous twinkle in his eyes, "Under the direction and to the satisfaction of the committee president, Mrs. Pruitt."

Junior winced.

"It's the only way I could keep her from suing your butts." Preacher Brown grinned.

Junior reached out for a departing handshake, but the preacher—apparently wanting to protect his hand from another bone-crunching grip—waved instead. "See you in church!" he said as he left the room.

Jo Massey

Toklat

Jo Massey

It was almost time for the evening campfire program to begin. From his relatively obscure viewpoint at the edge of the forest, Ranger Spencer Dunbar surveyed the group of thirty or so people getting settled, spreading their blankets and pillows on rough-hewed log benches placed in a semi-circle around the blazing campfire. Tourists mostly—men, women, and children—dressed in casual camp clothes, with cameras or binoculars slung around their necks, carrying bags containing sweaters, snacks, guide books, Denali Park souvenirs, maps of the Park, and tour bus schedules.

This far north in July, the arctic sun is above the horizon for over twenty hours each day, meaning that several hours of daylight still remained, making it hard to judge the time. Spencer glanced at his watch and a few minutes later—at precisely 7:30 p.m.—he stepped from the edge of the forest and walked to stand before the group of expectant people.

He knew that, in spite of the large black patch over his right eye, his looks never failed to impress. In fact, perhaps the patch, plus the long scar across his cheek, actually added an interesting flavor to his rugged appearance. A tall, well-built man in his late thirties, he was striking in his tailored green uniform. The wide brim of his hat, a loosely tied neckerchief around his throat, and slightly-longer-than-regulation sandy hair did a fair job of hiding the nasty scars on the back of his head and his neck.

As he approached the group, he noticed a young woman enter the circle and, after looking around for an available seat, she moved toward the front. His breath caught in his throat, and he felt a flush move up his face. Something about the self-confident way she moved, the turn of her head, the sway in her walk, her height and build, the cut of her hair—everything about her—made him believe for a moment that it was Monica.

Noticing his presence, the crowd quickly made final adjustments to their seating arrangements and sat eagerly awaiting his first words. Three pre-teen boys jostled one another for the best seat on the front row, but, still stunned at the woman's startling resemblance to Monica, Spencer scarcely saw them. Most nights one or more boys would sit gazing up at him with mesmerized expressions, and Spencer always suspected they each entertained dreams of becoming rangers themselves one day, just as he had when he was their age.

He cleared his throat. "Good evening, everyone. Thanks for coming tonight to learn more about Denali Park." As on other nights, he prepared to branch into a variety of facts and information that the tourists generally found interesting, including a discussion on the history of the famous mountain formerly known as Mount McKinley, now called Denali, or "Great One," by the area natives. Before continuing, he glanced at the young woman and saw that she was watching him with interest.

His presentation normally took about forty-five minutes, after which he allowed another fifteen minutes for questions and answers. Always, there were the inevitable questions about bears. Everyone is fascinated about the giant mammals that range Alaska—the black bears of the southeast with their blue-black coats, the enormous brown bears from the coastal regions, the fearsome white polar bears near the Arctic circle, the glacier bears living along ice fields; and, of course, the various sub-species of grizzlies, including the awe-inspiring blond Toklat bear often seen in the Park. The hope of seeing a bear is a big reason most folks visit Alaska, especially Denali Park since it was home to many of these impressive animals.

The questions would always eventually lead to him, no matter how hard he tried to skirt the subject, and he'd be forced to briefly explain about the patch; it came with the territory of being a ranger.

As he began his talk, he was acutely aware of the young woman, and he couldn't keep from looking at her. His gaze met her expressive, sparkling eyes, so similar to Monica's, yet not the same. She smiled a slow smile, and he was again startled at the uncanny resemblance. It unnerved him and he forgot what he was about to say. He looked away and tried to regain his composure. Unconsciously, he lifted the eye patch from his bad eye and rubbed the hollow socket—an unthinking habit he had developed and used when deep in thought—always done in privacy.

Shouts from the three boys jerked him from his reverie back into the present. "Yuk!" "Oh, gross!" "Creepy!" "Where's his eye?"

And in that moment he caught the startled look on her face. Only then did he realize what he had done—he had unveiled his hideous scar before the world, something he had kept safely hidden for three years.

The looks of adoration on the boys' young faces suddenly faded to horror and revulsion, quickly followed by a stronger emotion—curiosity. The three of them pushed forward, pressing close in front of him. "What happened to you?" they asked.

Stunned at their reaction, Spencer hesitated and was unable to find his voice to speak. He heard murmurs from the audience as he scanned their faces. Everyone seemed to want to avoid making eye contact with him, apparently embarrassed.

He understood the reaction of these people, remembering his own revulsion that moment in the hospital when the sympathetic doctor, who'd then left Spencer alone to make peace with his new face, had first handed him a mirror. The eye was gone. The socket, too badly damaged to even hold a false eye, had been sewn shut— a sunken, shriveled flap of skin without lashes, just stitched in a purple line from the bridge of his nose to the outer edge of the lid. Most of the eyebrow, too, was missing, replaced by an angry liver-colored scar, matching the line across his cheekbone. Plastic surgery hadn't been an option at the time, not until a deeper healing had been achieved and better surgical techniques had been developed. He was relegated to walk through life with the misshapen face of a freak—a monster.

Even though Spencer had anticipated that the sight of his face would have a profoundly negative effect on other people, now that it had happened he was uncharacteristically panicky and shaken. He couldn't find his voice to speak; he stood helplessly tongue-tied.

At that moment, he regretted his unintentional action and the stir it had caused. He was about to replace the patch when something made him hesitate. He'd often thought about trying to live without it, so perhaps this was the time. He would leave it off after all.

Two other rangers had wandered into the campfire circle just as this "unveiling" transpired. Dan Maxwell knew Spencer's story but he had never seen him without the patch. Larry Coe, on the other hand, knew the whole story intimately, because he had been there when it happened. Yet they never talked about the incident or about Monica. When they realized that Spencer was struggling for words, they hurried to where he stood and flanked their comrade.

Putting a hand on Spencer's shoulder, Larry said in a loud voice, "I believe there is a change in the program for tonight. Instead of talking about the park, we will discuss the dangers of rubbing up too close to a grizzly bear. You're in luck, because Ranger Dunbar is going to share his first-hand experience with all of us. When he's finished, you will know how to prevent such a horrible thing ever happening to you."

Dan joined in. "This is a personal story of bravery and survival that you will want to hear," he said. "And I guarantee, it's one that you'll never forget."

The three rangers captured the audience's interest immediately; this unusual beginning now appeared to have been deliberately planned and choreographed ahead of time. Some folks looked at Spencer a bit uneasily, but most expressions were a mix of curiosity and respect.

Word of the unusual spectacle spread throughout the campground and, as it did, the crowd swelled. After all the seats were filled, people continued to press in around the edges of the circle, getting as close as they could.

Spencer looked at the three boys on the front row and now saw gazes of awe and wonder on their upturned, eager faces. He looked at the young woman, afraid of seeing the revulsion he expected to find in her eyes, but she was smiling at him.

He'd wondered if he had done the right thing in leaving his grossly scarred face revealed. But it now appeared like it might turn out to be the impetus he'd needed, whether he consciously realized it or not. He began to relax.

So, on this summer evening, after those first awkward moments had passed, Spencer and his two companions gave one of the most unusual campfire presentations ever given. The audience—people representing countries from around the world—listened intently, mesmerized by the tale of adventure and misfortune.

The long siege of rain had finally ended when, on the fourth day after the Arctic sun came out, my two companions and I set out on a trip to the backcountry. Labor Day had come and gone and with it most of the tourists. Our official summer's duties as park rangers were nearly completed, yet still reluctant to leave the vast beauty and solitude of Denali, we each felt compelled to spend a few more days in that wilderness, absorbing as much of it as possible.

As the more seasoned of the three—my second summer working in Denali Park—I would be staying on for another month to help wind down the season before going back to Seattle, where I would spend the winter working on my first novel—so far a three-year unfinished project—and, to keep body and soul together, paint houses as a sub-contractor for my brother's construction company.

Larry was working on his master's degree in botany at the University of Idaho in Moscow and would be starting classes in another week. His first year as a park ranger had been a dream come true for him, and he'd fallen in love with the land. His intention after he'd earned his degree was to come back to live here; he hoped to teach at the University of Alaska in Fairbanks. I'd enjoyed working with Larry, who possessed an infectious optimism and positive attitude. At twenty-four and ten years my junior, he'd sometimes jokingly call me "Pop," to which I'd reciprocate with "Sonny."

The third person in our party was Monica. Ah, Monica. I'd been instantly attracted to her when she showed up in the office half an hour early for her appointment in a newly-issued park service uniform—so perfectly tailored to her figure as to be distracting—and her eyes glowing with excitement. She looked eighteen, not the twenty-eight her application indicated she was. She was slightly built, almost boyish in physique, but it didn't take long to figure out that she was physically strong and had a quick wit, which unfortunately could degenerate into a sharp tongue when she was provoked. She was a rookie, also, but when guiding a group of tourists, she spoke with such authority that no one would have ever believe she was new to the job. And no one would ever think to disagree with her proclamations or explanations or, if they did, they would likely go away with doubts about their own thoughts on the subject.

Almost immediately, Monica and I started seeing each other after hours, and now, as the time rapidly approached for us to go our separate ways, I was feeling sad. I was not looking forward to her return to her teaching job in St. Paul. This trip was to be the end of our summer together. I hoped our relationship could withstand the long months between now and next year's season and that it didn't prove to be the typical summer romance and no more.

"What's holding him up?" Monica paced back and forth beside our Park Service pickup, glancing now and then at her watch.

"It's only a quarter til," I reminded her. "We agreed to meet at seven. He'll be here by then."

She looked at me impatiently and continued her pacing. I'd learned that she made it a practice to arrive for any appointments at least half an hour ahead of time, and she seemed to believe everyone else should do the same. Her backpack was already loaded in the truck, and she was working on a second cup of coffee from her thermos. "Well, I hope so. The sun's already been up for nearly an hour. Times a wastin'!"

Feeling like an indulgent father, I smiled at her

impetuousness and thought how cute she looked in her jeans and hiking boots. She caught my stare and laughed impishly.

"Down, big boy," she said. "It's going to take all of today's energy just to get to tonight's camp. Don't get ideas." She glanced at her watch again and frowned.

"Hey there, Pop. Good morning, Monica." Larry thumped up the path and began shrugging out of his over-loaded backpack. "For once I'm early. A whole five minutes early." He grinned meaningfully at Monica, obviously aware that she had already begun fretting.

"Well, get that ridiculous thing loaded and let's get going," she said, as she climbed in and scooted to the middle seat.

Larry loaded his pack in the back and shrugged as he and I exchanged glances. I smiled and shook my head, then got in under the wheel. Choosing to ignore Monica's grouchiness, he slid into the passenger seat, slapped her lightly on a leg and said in his best John Wayne impression, "Well, little lady, I can't wait to get on the trail, can you?"

She glowered at him, and then broke into a smile. "No, I could hardly sleep last night, dreaming about this trip. Just think, five days to do nothing but wander around out there," she said, pointing through the windshield toward the towering mountains in the distance. "No lectures to give, no deadlines or timelines, nobody asking stupid questions. Only us three pitting our strength against all of nature."

It took an hour and half to drive the sixty miles to Stony Creek, where we parked the vehicle and unloaded our backpacks. Larry and I both had sturdy external frame packs, carrying about sixty-five pounds each, sharing the load of cooking equipment, tents, sleeping bags, an axe, small shovel and saw, and much of the food. Monica's pack weighed less—closer to fifty pounds; she was responsible for her sleeping bag, the lantern, eating utensils, and most of the perishable foods. We each had our own clothes, a compass, matches, emergency survival gear and other personal items. As an amateur photographer I also carried my 35 mm Canon camera with an assortment of lenses and a tripod.

We'd spent many hours with our heads bent over maps, planning our route. Unlike other national parks, there isn't a marked trail system here, so we'd be required to bushwhack the entire trip, much of which would lead through dense thickets of alder and willow and across boggy tundra— all difficult to navigate. This would make the going slow but would get us into country the average hiker never sees. Heading nearly due north, we'd skirt the western edge of Mt Sheldon and follow Stony Creek until it joined the Clearwater near a landing strip used by bush pilots and the old remnant of a ghost town, Stampede. From there we'd continue another three miles north to the confluence of the Toklat—an Indian name meaning "head of the water"—a glacial flat, half a mile wide, where the river spreads into many braided channels separated by huge gravel bars. There we'd turn southeast and follow the main Toklat River along the east side of Mt Sheldon back to the main road where it ends at Toklat Campground. We hoped to catch a ride from there for the remaining three miles to the pickup. We estimated the entire trip would cover about fifty-five miles.

It was an ambitious journey, but we had five days, which would only require an average of ten and a half miles a day, and we didn't anticipate having a problem with that, even though we expected the second leg of the trip to be more difficult, not knowing how many times we might have to cross parts of the larger river. However, on a positive note, with our food supplies dwindling daily with use, we'd be traveling with lighter packs by the time we got there.

"Help me finish up this coffee," Monica said as we got out. She filled the lid from the opened thermos and handed it to Larry.

"Don't mind if I do," he said, accepting it from her.

I opened a package of powdered sugar donuts. We each took one and then walked to the edge of the road and stood looking at the route we'd soon be taking. It would go through a meandering, tundra-meadowed valley stretching two or three miles to the north. Along the bottom, we could see the east branch of Stony Creek—not much more than a trickle this late in the season. In the distance, the shallow valley disappeared into a narrow canyon between two tree-covered hillsides, colorful in their autumn trappings.

"That's where things will start to get interesting," I said, pointing. "Once we get into the drainage we won't have to worry about getting lost. There's only one way through, as far as I can tell." I'd closely studied my maps and knew the most direct route was along the creek bottom.

Larry finished his coffee and Monica drained the thermos, refilling the lid for me. We each ate another donut; I downed the coffee, and we struggled into our packs.

"Okay, here we go," I said, glancing at my watch. "It's nine o'clock sharp. According to my map the best campsite potential is in the valley where Boundary Creek comes in, about nine miles out. "Even with breaks, we should be able to make that by early afternoon." I looked at my two companions and saw that they both had their packs on, fastened securely. They looked eager to get going.

Barely speaking, we walked single-file at a fairly brisk pace, getting accustomed to the weight of our packs and each searching, with not much success, to find some rhythm for crossing the uneven, spongy tundra—me in the lead, Monica next, Larry bringing up the rear.

At the end of the second mile, the east and west forks of Stony Creek joined. Monica and I waited for Larry to catch up. He'd stopped here and there to examine various species of plants growing in the lush tundra and to enter them in the journal he kept constantly with him. When he again joined us, his hiking boots were wet. He held out his hat to us. It was filled with dark fruit. "Here, I brought you a gift," he grinned. "There was a blueberry patch across the creek." From the looks of the bluish stains on his teeth, he'd eaten a hatfull by himself.

As we ate our fill of berries, we surveyed the terrain and decided to stay to the right side of the creek, which appeared to have less underbrush, offering the least resistance to traversing.

I started ahead, skirting the edge of the hill, and as I rounded a bend, I nearly stepped in a huge mound of bear scat, not yet a day old.

"Geez, would you look at this," I said.

"It looks like a giant blueberry pound cake," Monica said, glancing around nervously.

"I thought I saw signs of a bear working that patch

back there," Larry said. "A lot of the plants were trampled and matted down, probably where he laid down to sleep."

I took out my camera and snapped a couple of close-up pictures. "Yep. We really need to be on the lookout."

That bears were in this area was no surprise. We knew that, of course. Each of us had often seen them when we'd traveled out on one of the tour buses. But, from the window of a bus they look benign, like giant stuffed toys—cute, cuddly, often comical—especially a pair of cubs at play, or a boar chasing a ground squirrel he'd just dug out of its hole, pouncing on it as it tries to escape his deadly claws. The light colored Toklat grizzly—sometimes referred to as "blond" grizzly—is abundant in this region of the Park.

At the campfire talks I gave during the summer I generally talked a lot about bears—how unpredictable they are, stressing their size and strength, how fast they can run, how potentially dangerous they are, especially when they have cubs with them. I was sometimes amused by the serious wide-eyed looks of terror I saw on the faces of my audiences as their imaginations take over.

"Time to make a lot of racket to let them know we're here," I reminded the other two. "They don't want to bump into us any more than we want to bump into them."

"I'll sing," Monica said.

"Oh, lord, please don't," Larry teased. "They might be tempted to kill you, just to be rid of the atrocious sound."

Monica stuck out her tongue at him and he laughed. She pushed passed me, taking the lead. She began singing *Blueberry Hill* at the top of her lungs. "*I found my thrillllllll, on Blueberry Hillllllllll...*"

I looked back at Larry. He winked and, so she would be sure to hear, he yelled, "May God preserve us."

She ignored him and continued, *"on Blueberry Hill, when I found you...."*

Before long, Monica stopped singing and started swearing. We'd come to a nearly impenetrable dense thicket of scrub willow and alders. The trees, which had appeared beautiful in their fall hues, now seemed sinister. None of the three choices for getting past this obstacle were ideal—take to the creek, narrow and deep, with a very rocky bottom at this point, or scramble up the side of the steep hill, or burrow straight through the thicket. Each option seemed equally formidable.

I voted that we push our way through the thicket, but the other two had their own ideas about the best choice.

"I'm going up and around," Monica said. "At least I'll be able to see."

Larry opted for the creek since his boots were already wet.

Before I got even halfway through the snarl of trees, I wished I'd gone either of the other routes. Here the alders have an irritating habit of growing limbs close to the ground and then spaced at uneven heights up their entire trunk, making it impossible to walk through standing erect. I'd step over a yawning low branch, only to have one of the branches above snag on my pack or the leg of my tripod, yanking me backward. I'd back step, hunch over, try to compress myself into a smaller package, which, with the weight distribution of my pack, would throw me off balance; then I'd attempt it again. Over and over I repeated this exercise—two steps forward, one back.

"Spence, where are you?" I heard Larry yelling from somewhere in front of me.

"I heard him a ways back, crashing through the brush and squawking like a camp-robber," I heard Monica tell him.

"I'm coming," I shouted, then swore as another branch reached out and grabbed my pack, nearly toppling me to my knees. When I finally reached them, I was irritated and exhausted.

"Well, I'm sure glad we chose you as our leader," Monica said sarcastically. "Even more glad I decided not to follow your lead."

I didn't feel like humoring her with a reply so ignored it by taking a long drink from my canteen. I noticed Larry's pant legs were wet to the knees and Monica's elbow was oozing blood.

"What happened to your arm?" I asked.

She pretended she didn't know what I was talking about. "Oh, this little scratch? It's nothing."

"Really?" I took her arm and looked at it. It was only a superficial scrape, but needed to be tended. I opened my pack and took out the first aid kit. "Here let me put this on it," I said. I applied a layer of antibacterial ointment, and then covered it with an adhesive bandage. "Okay, tell me how that happened."

"I just slipped. My foot gave way and I scraped it on a rock. That's all."

I raised an eyebrow. "You implied your way was a piece of cake."

She tossed her head and shrugged. "It had an occasional

rough spot, but I still think my way was the best way."

"There was an undercurrent of difficulty with the river route, too," Larry joked, obviously enjoying his pun.

"I'll have to agree any way would have been better than the mad scramble through the brambles," I said. We all laughed.

Larry took point, and we continued working our way along the creek, making painfully slow progress. Repeatedly we came to areas similar to the one just past, but as the creek turned westward, passage became easier—either the creek was shallower and more passable, or the route around, or through, the stand of willows and alders was gentler.

By four o'clock, the hill to our left began to drop away, revealing another open rolling-tundra meadow. Here Boundary Creek joined Stony Creek, and we set up camp on a low knoll situated in the juncture between the two.

We were all three tired, so we laid down in our tents for an hour before starting supper—Larry in his, Monica and me in mine.

I was up first. I started a fire, boiled water for tea, heated a couple of cans of beef stew, and set out the hardtack. The smell of hot food woke the other two, and I heard grunts and moans as they crawled out of the tents.

"Ummm, smells good," Monica said, yawning and stretching. She'd put on a light jacket. "What can I do to help?"

"You can do the dishes after we eat," I replied.

"Ugh, you know I hate doing dishes."

"Sorry, but everybody has to share the work. Can't be like the Little Red Hen's friends out here," I said, knowing she wasn't serious, or even if she were, that she'd do her part.

"I'll get more wood," Larry said and went in search of some. I knew he really wanted to check out the flora. He returned with one armload of wood and a fist full of plant stems, just as the food was ready to dish up.

"There are lots of interesting tracks along the water's edge," he said. "I saw some fairly good sized lynx prints in among what I'd guess to be fox, and some smaller tracks that are possibly weasel."

After Monica had washed the supper dishes, we stuffed everything, except sleeping needs, into our packs, and then Larry and I hauled them back across the creek to hoist them into the tallest tree we could find—a preventative measure to keep any marauding animals from coming into camp or scavenging our supplies.

Before crawling into our tents for the night, we discussed plans for tomorrow. We chose the landing strip near Stampede—approximately a fourteen-mile hike—as the goal for our next camp. Knowing we needed to get a much earlier start, we retired early.

We were on the trail shortly after the sun came up just before six. The second day went pretty much as the first—numerous battles with alders and willows, areas of spongy tundra, creek crossings, scrambles up the sides of hills flanking the river as it coursed its way to join Clearwater Creek.

Shortly after four in the afternoon, we sighted—coming in from our left—the larger river on the far side of an alluvial valley and, just ahead on a sand bar, the landing area. The watercourse we'd follow tomorrow was triple the size of the creek where we'd begun our journey, and the increase in size was already impressive. I was eager, yet somewhat apprehensive, to see the volume where these waters would marry into the Toklat.

Exhausted from the long day's tramp, we dropped our packs, pitched the tents, and decided to wait until morning to explore the ghost town. We ate a cold supper, hung our packs, and crawled stiffly into our sleeping bags, even before the sun had set.

I woke with stiff muscles, but feeling refreshed, just as the first streaks of morning light scattered the night shadows. I dressed quietly so as not to wake Monica and then crawled from the tent.

The morning was clear and crisp. It was one of those rare mornings without any clouds obscuring the crown of Denali towering majestically fifty miles to the southwest. The pre-dawn twilight transformed the snowy peak, making it look like a monolithic granite cake with pink icing slathered into every crook and cranny. The view was spectacular, the color fleeting. I hurriedly set up my tripod and took several pictures. Even as I did, the pallet of color switched from that first pink to rose, to ruby, to claret, to vermilion. I shot up the rest of the roll of film in my camera, hoping to capture the essence of the changing mood of the mountain.

The overwhelming scene made me feel insignificant and humbled. In the face of such aged grandeur, I was acutely aware of man's irrelevance and mortality. Yet, by some strange force, the mountain also filled me with a sense of expansiveness, as if it somehow imparted to me some of its strength, making me feel enlarged—like I could take on the world.

I stretched, yawned, then wandered back to camp, started a fire, and retrieved our packs from where we'd stashed them in the tree the night before. Having decided ahead of time that we'd only try to cover nine miles today, I let the others sleep until seven and woke them when the coffee was ready. We took our time with breakfast, making pancakes and scrambled eggs from powered mixes.

After we'd finished eating, we explored the remnants of the old ghost town. Nothing much remained to tell of the men who'd lived here, lured by hopes and dreams of personal wealth to be had in the antimony mines. We wondered if many succeeded in making that dream come true. A few hand-hewed logs were scattered about, marking where a building or two had once stood, but there was nothing that would even make an interesting souvenir.

Larry wandered off to gather flora data, while Monica and I cleaned up the dishes and broke camp. I could see Larry stooped over examining the tundra, scribbling entries in his notebook. As I watched, he stood up and glanced around. He suddenly waved to get my attention, then pointed across the river, up the Clearwater Creek valley floor. A half-mile away a couple of hundred caribou were grazing, unconcerned by our presence.

I took Monica's hand and we walked to the edge of the river. "There's something I've been wanting to talk to you about," I said.

She looked up at me and seemed about to make some flippant remark, then changed her expression. "Okay," she said. "What is it?"

"I'd like for you to come with me to Seattle. I have a little house there. It isn't much, but we could look for a bigger place if you didn't like it. You could probably get a teaching job there if you wanted to work, or you could just stay at home and relax, read, write—whatever pleases you." I blurted this out almost without stopping to take a breath, all the time watching her expression for some clue to her reaction. "I can't stand the thought of not seeing you again until next year, or worse, never seeing you again. I'm really crazy about you, Monica. Please say yes."

She lowered her eyes from my face and was quiet for a long moment. When she spoke, she said, "I can't, Spencer. You know how much I love my teaching job and besides, all my family is back there in Minnesota. I couldn't drop everything just like that and go running off to Seattle. Nobody would understand. That would be very irresponsible of me."

"I thought maybe you'd begun to love me a little," I fumbled.

"I do love you. But I'm not ready for that kind of commitment," she said. "We'll be together again next summer. And I'll write—every day if you want. Maybe we can get together occasionally—over the holidays or during my spring break. I could fly to Seattle, or you could come to Minnesota." She spoke rapidly, as if she'd anticipated my proposal and had rehearsed this speech ahead of time.

I felt sharp disappointment and knew it must show in my eyes. I dropped her hand and turned to face the river. I waited, hoping she would touch me, would tell me she'd already changed her mind, or at least that she would think about it before giving me a final no. But all I heard were her footsteps crossing the gravel back to our camp.

When Larry returned, we donned our backpacks and began the day's trek. As we headed north, the watercourse divided into a series of channels, braiding back and forth across a wide, flat riverbed. We chose a path leading along the gravel bar on the outer bank of the channel to the east, which seemed to be clearer of obstacles for the foreseeable distance. We would run into the convergence of the Clearwater and Toklat in about six miles—the furthest point of our trip—and from there begin the return journey back along the latter.

"Who wants to lead?" I asked.

Monica gave me a look I didn't understand and shrugged. "I'll do it if you don't want to," she said and started past me. I reached to take her hand, but she jerked it away and pushed by. "Just try to keep up." Her tone sounded sarcastic as she strode off at a fast clip.

"What the heck's gotten into her this morning?" Larry asked. "I guess I'll never understand women."

"Well, Sonny, I suppose she's started her period or something," I said, trying to make my voice sound light.

"Oh, lord. That's just what we need—a bleeding woman out here in bear country!"

He was right, and I hoped that my cynical assessment wasn't actually the case. Not wanting to divulge my earlier conversation with her, I'd given that trite explanation for her actions as a joke. I couldn't understand why she was angry with me for my proposal, but it had obviously upset her.

Monica walked at such a fast clip, she was half a mile ahead of us before she reached a point where the channel cut sharply to the right bank, blocking further travel on the gravel bar. When we caught up to her, she still looked angry, but now her frustration was about this new impediment to our progress.

It was too dangerous to safely ford there—the water dropped immediately from the bank into a deep trough. We backtracked several hundred yards but only found one spot that, even though the river was considerably further across at this point, seemed shallow enough for us to attempt a crossing. I judged the distance to be about thirty yards.

We sat down, removed our hiking boots and socks, then crammed the socks into the tops of our packs so we'd have dry ones to put back on when we reached the other side. Then we put the boots back on, so we'd have protection from sharp rocks as we crossed.

"Unsnap your packs," I commanded. "That'll make them easier to ditch in case, God forbid, you fall in and have to swim for your life." I tied one end of a rope around my waist and passed it back to Monica. She also fastened a loop around herself and tossed the other end to Larry, who tied the other end securely around himself.

I stepped into the flow and found bottom when the water reached my hips. The current wasn't too swift, but the bottom was rocky, making each step tricky. It was impossible to see through the milky glacial water, so I moved slowly, searching for solid footing. I took several steps, and then, glancing over my shoulder, motioned for Monica to follow. She looked scared, but sat down on the bank, then slid both feet in at the same time until she was submerged in water above her waist.

"Yikes," she yelled as it hit her midriff. "This is colder than Yeti's balls." She struggled to lift her pack higher onto her shoulders in a futile attempt to keep the bottom of it from getting soaked. Her sleeping bag would have to be dried out before going to bed.

Larry followed her into the river and we moved slowly across the expanse. In the middle, I began to feel dizzy and disoriented—hypnotized by the motion of flowing water—and stopped to look to the opposite shore to regain my sense of equilibrium.

"What's the hold up?" Monica said, standing directly behind me. "Let's get out of here. I'm freezing my ass off!"

I moved ahead without glancing back, forcing myself to look away from the water every few steps, and felt relief each time the distance to the gravel bar diminished. The water was much shallower the last few yards, and it was a relief to have solid ground beneath my feet.

We dumped the water and silt out of our boots, and quickly replaced our wet clothes with dry ones from our packs.

"Let's take a break," I said.

"Good idea," they both agreed, and we flopped down on the sand. Monica pulled three Baby Ruth candy bars from her pack and handed us each one. We ate without speaking; perhaps, each in our own way, we were quietly giving thanks that we'd had no mishaps.

We still had three miles to hike before we'd reach the Toklat, and I worried about how many more channel crossings of this river would be required before we got to the juncture— let alone how many we'd have to make on the Toklat itself.

But, fortunately, as it turned out, we only had to cross twice more, and both times the channels were shallow enough to ford easily without aid of the rope. There was only the tiresome ritual of removing our socks each time, then dumping icy water and grainy silt out of the boots before putting the dry socks back on; time consuming, but sensible.

As we approached the confluence, we scrambled up a steep bank, forced our way through yet another thick stand of willow, and emerged at last on a bluff overlooking the marriage of the two bodies of water where they collided below us. Near the top, we had another spectacular view of Denali, an ethereal glistening white monarch towering above the more somber hues of crimson and gold that told of autumn.

We decided to take a much-deserved break on this warm grassy point. While Monica made sandwiches, I opened her sleeping bag and spread it across a thicket of dwarf birch, hoping it would dry in the noonday sun.

Over lunch we talked about the hardships of the trip so far—the river crossings, the frustrations of getting through unwieldy growths of trees, the difficulties of walking on spongy, uneven tundra, the scrapes, bruises, sore and aching muscles, and blistered feet. We joked about our individual foibles and oddities—my ability to pick the most difficult route and my lack of balance crossing the river—Larry's ever-growing collection of flora growing above the permafrost, such as several species of sedges, a variety of mosses, blueberry and numerous other plants—Monica's colorful and profane language. "Cold as Yeti's balls? If you knew anything about a male, you'd know that's the one area that adapts to make sure it stays warm," Larry teased.

I remember that conversation as if it were yesterday. But my memory is unclear about the exact sequence of events after that—they all happened so fast.

Monica went to look for blueberries and to "find a tree." She'd gone down the slope towards the river. Larry had wandered into the forest on his insatiable quest for some new exotic species of plant. I'd taken my camera and tripod and was heading back to that clearing where we'd seen Denali in hope of getting photos from this angle and in this light.

Then she screamed. I do remember that scream—will remember it as long as I live. Shrill and clear, pure terror. A second shriek, "Bear!"

I began to run towards the sound. My feet pumped, yet my body seemed to move in slow motion as if I were in one of those nightmares I sometimes have where I feel like I'm running in place.

When at last I reached the clearing, what I saw made my blood freeze. Fifty yards away Monica was curled into a ball on the ground, a Toklat grizzly pawing her like she was a ground squirrel. Looking on curiously from the edge of the trees was a yearling cub.

My fear for her life filled me with a rage I've never known before. The vehemence of it seemed to take control of my mind and body, filling me with unbelievable boldness. Without thought or plan, I charged down the slope in full attack, swinging my tripod over my head. I heard a hideous, primal caterwaul—the sound so close it could only have come from me, yet so unearthly in tone it seemed impossible that it could have.

As I got close the bear stopped tearing at Monica. It

reared up on its hind legs and faced me. It swung its mammoth head from side to side, looking at me.

Blood seemed to be everywhere—blood soaking through Monica's shirt, blood already matting in her hair, blood dripping from the bear's claws, blood staining its snout and the furry ruff around its head. I saw it all through the blood of murder in my own eye.

Fueled by fear of losing Monica to this creature and crazed with hatred for it, I rushed in, flailing my inept weapon, brandishing it with all the force I could muster. My ineffectual blows to the sow's head and broad chest did—as I hoped it would—turn the bear's focus from Monica to me. I swung repeatedly, striking blindly, and screaming my battle cry. The bear slowly raised one paw is if to ward off my blows and then, like a heavy weight boxer, it struck so fast with its other paw I didn't see it coming—only felt the force of it.

Before losing consciousness, the last thing I remembered was the agony of a bone-crushing blow to my head that spiraled me into the air, then the jarring landing as I crumpled to the ground. I was aware of pain in my eye and of my own blood pumping down my cheek. Then I slipped into darkness.

During the evening's campfire talk, Larry had effectively summarized the rescue for the crowd of mesmerized tourists. He told how, that after pitching a tent and wrapping the two wounded victims in sleeping bags to help protect them and giving whatever emergency aid he could, he'd made his own mad marathon up the Toklat. He traveled light and kept moving all afternoon into the evening and all night, stopping only for brief periods of rest, making the difficult twenty-two miles in a record eleven hours. Luckily, a small crew of park service employees had just arrived to begin working at Toklat Campground when he arrived, and they radioed headquarters for help.

In the telling of his story to the group of visitors, Spencer hadn't included the parts of his involvement with and proposition to Monica. That was private business and he didn't want to share that with anyone, especially strangers.

After the talk was finished, many people came to shake his hand, sincere in their words of empathy. The little boys, eyes shining with admiration, hung around until their parents made them come away.

When the crowd was gone, Spencer slumped onto one of the vacant benches. He was exhausted, drained by the emotions of the evening and relieved it was over. He felt liberated, yet still empty—liberated finally from some of the emotional wounds, empty because something was still missing. He knew the vacancy left by Monica's silence would never be filled. He'd never been able to understand why she'd never answered any of his letters or returned any of his phone calls.

Larry came and sat beside him. "I think that went well," he said cheerfully.

"I don't know," Spencer said. "That was an unthinking and stupid thing for me to do."

"So, why did you?" Larry asked.

Spencer considered the question before revealing the

truth. "Did you see that woman sitting near the front, over on the left?"

Larry looked at him closely. "Yes, the one that looked a little like Monica? She reminded me of her, too."

"When I saw her come in, I thought for a minute that it was Monica. It startled me at first, and then suddenly it was three years ago and I was with her again. I forgot where I was. Rubbing that spot has become a subconscious habit, I guess."

After a long pause Larry said, "I've wondered if you would ever stop hiding behind that mask." There was compassion in his voice.

Spencer looked at his friend for a long moment before answering. "I wear the patch to protect other people from having to see my gross scars," he said in self-defense.

Larry gazed into Spencer's good eye without flinching and didn't respond, silently but clearly challenging this excuse.

Finally, Spencer lowered his gaze and his voice. "No, I guess maybe you're right. I have been hiding, and I'm tired of it. I'm tired of feeling ashamed of how I look. Tired of being alone. I yearn for companionship, yet I know I'll never be able to attract another woman."

"Ummm, feeling sorry for ourselves, are we?" Larry laid his hand on Spencer's shoulder and gave it a friendly squeeze.

The two men sat quietly for several minutes. Finally Spencer took the black patch from his pocket and twisted it between his fingers, turning it over and over, as if trying to decide whether to put it on or leave it off.

"I saw her last winter," Larry suddenly said.

Spencer flinched and immediately stopped playing with the patch. "You mean Monica?" he asked. He didn't look at his friend.

"Yes, Monica. She made me promise not to tell you, but I think you should know," Larry continued. "She and I have kept in touch every since the accident. She always asks about you."

There was a long pause as Spencer tried to digest this information. "How is she?" he finally asked.

"She's doing well. Still teaching in St. Paul. Never married. She's more beautiful than ever, sweeter tempered even, less caustic." Larry chuckled. "Remember how grumpy she was that day?"

"Yes, I remember," Spencer said. "I replay that day over and over in my mind, and wonder what I could have done differently. I think she's held me responsible for what happened, and I do feel guilty sometimes. I should have been able to protect her better."

"It wasn't your fault. It wasn't anybody's fault," Larry said. "It's one of those things that happens—almost to be expected by people like us, who spend lots of time in the wilderness. Besides, you shouldn't feel that way. I know that Monica doesn't hold you responsible."

"I wish I could believe that. I guess I should just be happy that she survived. I am, of course. I might have had a chance with her before I got this ugly mug. I only wish things could have ended up different for us."

"I know," Larry sympathized.

"How badly scarred did she ended up?" Spencer asked.

"Her only physical scars are on her back, where they

aren't visible. But, I'm afraid she has as many scars as you on the inside," Larry said sadly.

"Scars on the inside? What do you mean?"

"You obviously believe she doesn't want to have anything to do with you because of your looks, or maybe you think she hates you because you let it happen," Larry said.

"Well, I do. Isn't that true?"

"The truth is she thinks she doesn't deserve you. She's convinced that it was her fault. She feels guilty that she's the one responsible for you having had to suffer all..." Larry trailed off, then pointed to Spencer's scarred face. "All of that," he finished.

"That's crazy. I had to try to save her life. It didn't matter what happened to me. I loved her."

"She's always said it happened because she wasn't watching where she was going that day—said if she'd been alert she should have seen the bear or the cub, should have known she was wandering in between them."

"That's ridiculous. We both know sometimes it's impossible to see anything in that brush, especially anything lying down."

"I know. That's what I told her. Yet all this time she's continued to insist that it happened because of her negligence. She said she wasn't paying attention, because she was so deep in thought about a conversation the two of you'd had earlier."

"Oh," Spencer said. "I see." He slowly put the patch over his eye. Hesitatingly he asked, "Did she tell you that I wanted her to come live with me in Seattle?"

"No, she didn't say exactly, but I assumed it was something like that," Larry said. "It's been very hard for me to stand back and watch the two of you—both of you being so stubborn in your pride and self-pity—especially when I feel a loyalty to both of you. That's why I haven't said anything to you about it before. But tonight it seems like the thing to do."

The two rangers stood and began walking towards their quarters. "Thanks for stepping in tonight," Spencer said. "I didn't anticipate things getting out of hand as they did, and I really needed your help." He extended his hand to his friend. "And thanks for telling me about Monica. You've given me much to think about."

Larry grinned and shook his hand. "You're welcome, Pop," he said.

Spencer smiled at Larry's use of the old term. "Goodnight, Sonny," he said and turned towards his room.

Larry stopped before his own door across the hall. With his hand resting on the knob, he looked back at Spencer.

"You know, Spence," he said, "I have a feeling that if you asked her again, Monica would have a different answer."

Spencer couldn't sleep. The scenes of the evening, the flashbacks to that fateful trip, and Monica's face kept flashing on the screen of his mind. After struggling with himself, he finally made a decision.

It was after three in the morning in Minnesota, but he called anyway. The sleepy voice on the other end answered, "Hello?"

"Monica?" His voice choked. "It's Spencer."

There was a long pause, and he realized she was crying. Then she was laughing. They talked for two hours, their conversation soon sliding into the easy rapport they'd always enjoyed. It seemed like the silence of the three long years since that fateful day had not really existed.

As they said goodnight, she started to hum. He recognized the Brook Benton tune even before she began to softly sing the words, *"...though we're apart, you're part of me still, for you were my thrill on Blueberry Hill."*

He'd never heard anything sweeter. "I love you, Monica."

"I love you, too."

Cabin Fever

Jo Massey

It was two in the morning when the door to Shorty's Bar burst open, forming a cloud of fog where frigid outside air met the heated atmosphere of the room. Charlie staggered in. The few patrons still there ignored him completely. His characteristic shuffle had turned to a kind of stumbling gallop. His Aleut Indian eyes, normally squinty, were wide open revealing bloodshot veins and muddy brown irises.

"You never guess what I just seen," he blurted excitedly.

"What? Your shadow?" one of the men at the bar said, laughing rudely.

"Naw, he probably sobered up enough to realize we got eighteen feet of new snow since the last time he was sober," another man answered the first. The group at the bar turned back to their drinks.

"Come on, guys," Charlie whined. "It's maybe important."

Still they ignored him. He stood swaying and blinking

in the middle of the room. "Bastards," he muttered to himself.

Dan, the bartender on duty, looked at Charlie but quickly turned back to the TV and pretended to be heavily engrossed in an old *Gunsmoke* rerun. He'd refused to serve Charlie earlier in the evening and had sent him away.

A commercial came on. Charlie's eyes stabbed at the back of Dan's head.

"Hey! Hey! Hey!" he said, using the words like a stiff finger poking at Dan's brain.

"Dammit, Charlie, I already told you I can't sell you any more booze tonight. Go home and sober up."

"But you don't understand. I seen something's maybe very, very important," he said, flinging his arms wide dramatically, nearly falling over with the abrupt movement.

"Ye gods!" Dan said wearily, aware the others were watching the action with sidelong glances. "What on earth did you see that's got you so excited?"

"I'm down by the dock, see. Mindin' my own business," he started.

"Yeah, right, the business of getting smashed," someone hissed in a loud whisper and there were giggles around the room.

Charlie glared at them. "Bastards," he muttered again. He looked pleadingly into Dan's face. "Just one beer, okay? I need it bad."

The sound of rifle fire and grunts from dying bad guys were heard on the TV. "No, dammit, get on with it. I'm missing out on *Gunsmoke*," Dan said.

Charlie looked disappointed, and then went on with

his story. "Like I was sayin', I'm down by my skiff. I think I hear sumpin'. I look up on the wharf. Can't hardly see nothin' through the snow. But someone's there. I look hard. Then I see woman's legs. Long, white legs, in a real short dress. High heels, too. Christ! Maybe Dan's right—I am drunk. Must be a vision, I think. Marilyn Monroe come to haunt me."

"Sure, Charlie, sure. Marilyn Monroe," one of the men said.

"Yeah, right," another man piped up. "Dan, why don't you call the sheriff's office and see if they'll send someone over to take him home?" Everyone laughed.

"No. It's true. Really," he protested. "She runs down the dock. Then I don't see her no more. I follow her. I get to end of the dock. I don't see nothin'. Then I hear sumpin'. I gotta wipe snow out of my eyes. I look way down at the ocean and see her movin' down there."

The patrons of the bar, displaying mild interest, began to gather around Charlie. After all, a woman wearing a dress in a small Alaskan fishing town was something to talk about—let alone wearing a dress in a near blizzard, on a shipping dock in the middle of the night. "What was she doing?" Dan asked.

"Was she drowning?" someone else asked.

"Drowning?" Charlie said, convulsing in a giggle.

"No, stupid, she weren't drowning. How c'ud she drown? The tide's out." Charlie sniffed disdainfully at the man he'd called bastard earlier.

There was a long pause while everyone waited for more. Finally, another man asked impatiently, "Well? So?

What happened?"

Charlie surveyed his now attentive audience with a look of satisfaction. "There's this woman—in mud up to here." He swiped a hand across mid-thigh. "I think maybe nobody tell'd her about our tides." His leathery faced cracked into a knowledgeable grin.

"Go on. Then what?" Dan prodded.

"It's her screamin' I heard. Screamin' and bawlin'. Mad screamin', like my old lady when I come home drunk. Like probably she will when I get home tonight." Charlie stopped speaking and seemed to go into sort of a reverie. "If I go home," he muttered more or less to himself.

"Only time I heard your wife scream at you she wasn't just screaming. She was yelling all sorts of stuff," Dan said with a grin. "Things better left unsaid in polite company."

"Same's this'n," Charlie declared. "She was yellin' stuff awright!"

"Like what?" Dan asked, looking at the folks gathered around the Indian. They all seemed interested now.

"Well, like 'How can anybody stand livin' in this hell hole. I hate it, hate it.' Then she was screaming, 'I'd rather be dead than live here in this goddamn mother....' " Charlie stopped before completing the expletive. "Well, she didn't 'xactly say it like that. Said she'd rather be dead than have to stay here another minute," he finished lamely.

There was silence in the bar except for Miss Kitty's gravely voice offering Marshall Dillon a drink. Everyone's eyes were focused on the town drunk.

"Maybe she's mostly mad 'cause she jumped off the

wrong side of the dock," Charlie said. "Long ways down there to get only mud. Twenty-five feet. Maybe thirty."

"Well, it's a damn good thing she didn't jump off the leeward side!" Dan said. "She'd have drowned for sure."

Charlie looked slightly aggravated for the interruption. He cleared his throat importantly and continued. "So I yell down, 'What'sa matter, lady?' She acts like she's mad at me. Tries to throw mud balls at me. 'What you think you're lookin' at?' she screams."

"So, then what did you do?"

"I came here. Think maybe I should tell someone."

"Good God, man! Do you mean she's still down there?" Dan gasped. "She'll die of exposure!"

Within five minutes of the first wailing of the civil defense siren, the little town was alive. A light was on in every house. Vehicle engines could be heard running in the frosty air. Voices shouting from one neighbor to another, "Some damn woman tried to commit suicide at the dock."

Jim Muldoon was among the first volunteer firemen to arrive on the scene. He shined his high-beam flashlight through the falling snow and around the muddy tidal flat until he saw her. Her upper torso was slumped over and she was holding herself in convulsive shivering. A sliver of the white flesh of her leg was barely visible above the edge of the watery goo. He could see that the report had been correct. It was a woman in a skirt. She was wearing only a waist-length fur jacket. Jim knew she couldn't live long in these conditions.

"Hurry up with that crane, Mike," he yelled, as a black power wagon slammed to a stop a few feet away. "Can you swing the boom around to this side?"

"Sure can. You going to ride 'er down to get the gal?"

"Yes. We should be able to pull her right out. I'm just worried about the tide coming back in on us. You know how fast it can move in and it's already starting to advance. It's up to within about five feet of her already. You got a blanket with you?"

"In the truck," Mike answered. He was already climbing into the cab of the crane and in moments it shuddered awake.

Vehicles and people were suddenly crawling over the dock. Voices, raised to be heard over the crane, shouted questions to one another.

"What's going on?"

"It's a woman. Look there."

"What's she doing down there?"

"Damned if I know. Musta tried to kill herself."

"Who is she? She ain't from here!"

"I bet she's one of the passengers from the plane."

"Oh, you mean the one that's been stuck here for two or three weeks. That makes sense."

"Yeah. This blasted storm hasn't let up enough to let it take off again."

"Don't look like it ever intends to either. I'm about sick to death of it myself," Betty Russell said. She had just arrived and from the way she was dressed she was prepared to stay for the long term—Carhartt coveralls, huge white bunny boots, beaver parka with it's voluminous hood pulled tight around her face, a ski mask, and fur mittens.

Everyone crowded around the edge of the dock to get a better look at the rescue operation. The boom of the shipping crane was carefully lowered the thirty-some-feet down to where the woman remained glued to the floor of the ocean.

Jim rode down on the hook, but it was immediately obvious that if he took a step off he would be in the same predicament as the woman. He tried to get a response from her but there was none. He wrapped the blanket about her shaking frame. "Pull me back up," he hollered to Mike.

Someone grabbed an empty shipping crate and it was quickly loaded down with a stout harness, more blankets, flashlight, and a thermos of coffee. Jim climbed in and began the descent again. His fear grew for the still form of the woman below him. He didn't know for sure how long she had been exposed to the elements, but he knew all too well how quickly life could ease away in the harsh world he called home. Even though he was accustomed to dealing with unusual rescues and had grown somewhat calloused to seeing death, he didn't want to see this woman die.

Thoughts raced through Jim's mind. Darn that Charlie, anyway! If he'd stay off the sauce, maybe he would've had enough sense to go to the sheriff's office first and bought them a little more time. But, then, if Charlie hadn't been down here looking for another bottle of booze in his skiff, he wouldn't have seen her and she would have died for sure—disappeared in the next tide. No one would have even missed her, no one from here anyway. Surely a family somewhere would have eventually wondered. But, as Robert Service so poetically put it, "there are strange things done in the midnight sun." Persons missing in Alaska are not rare occurrences—often, because no one knows to, they are never even searched for—just another mystery. He shook off the tragic thought.

There was still no response from the woman when Jim called to her. Fear tugged at him. "Just hang in there, Lady," he called. "I'm coming. We'll get you out of here in no time."

The water had reached her now and was lapping up her right side, causing her body to sway slightly with its rhythmic ebb and flow.

"Don't go dying on me now, you hear?" he pleaded softly as he reached her.

He uncoupled the box from the crane line. It sank into the mud a few inches, then held steady. He wrapped another blanket around her still body and pressed his fingers to her jugular vein. Yes, there was a faint pulse. Releasing a slow breath in relief, he lifted her limp arms and looped the harness rope under them, letting them drop again. Then, without looking up, he pumped his thumb upward to signal the crane to lift. The water was rising quickly. "Pull, Mike. Hurry!"

The harness lifted against her arms, hiking them up until it looked like they would pull out of her shoulder joints, but the rest of her body did not move. "Hold on," Jim yelled, raising a clenched fist to indicate STOP.

The line went slack, and Jim re-adjusted the rope around her chest, then wrapped his arms around the slender waist. He released one hand just long enough to signal Mike to lift again. He pulled with the crane, straining against the force of the mud that would suck her deeper as the tidal flow moved about them. "Come on. Help me save you," he said, breathing against the head leaning loosely on his chest.

Mike was an artist with the crane. He applied just the right amount of pressure, and with the help of Jim's steady tug, the woman was pulled free of the grip of black sticky gumbo. The sounds on the dock became still as all eyes were fixed on the slim figure rising through a curtain of falling snow. It was like watching a movie in slow motion.

"I'll be damned, it does look like Marilyn Monroe in that movie where her dress blows over her head," Dan said to the men from the bar. "Charlie was right. Where is he, anyway?"

"Went home to sleep it off, I guess," someone answered. "I see his wife over there and he isn't with her, so he must have taken the opportunity to sneak in while she's out here."

The ambulance didn't really need the siren and lights to clear the way to the clinic. The only person not on the wharf was Doctor Blevins, ready and waiting for his patient.

"Come on up to the cafe," Betty called to the rescuers as she headed her stout frame towards her truck. "I'll get the coffee going." She turned to another woman in the crowd of onlookers. "Why don't you come with me, Gladys? We'll feed these big, brave, strong men some good breakfast." She threw a familiar teasing glance to where the men stood.

They laughed good-naturedly at her comfortable joking. "Make it snappy, Old Broad," one of them shouted back. "We'll be right there."

Betty's Cafe was bursting with conversation when Jim came in after leaving the clinic. All eyes turned to meet his. "Well?" they all seemed to ask.

"Doc says she's not in real good shape, but he thinks

she's going to live. He's getting her stabilized. Warming her up gradually. Said it's a good thing she wasn't out there any longer or it would have been curtains for sure."

"Who is she, anyway? Did you find that out?"

"Well, another woman stranded on the same plane came to the clinic. She said this gal was sharing a room with her at the hotel. Her name is Francine Lewis. She was going home to San Diego from Anchorage. Her boss had her take this milk run flight so she could drop off some papers to one of the senators in Juneau."

"Wow. She must have an important job if her boss is dealing with a senator."

"I asked the other woman, but she didn't know. All she knew was that being stranded here for days, now weeks, on end with nothing to do but drink coffee and play solitaire was getting to this woman pretty bad."

Betty stood looking ruefully out at the falling snow. "Well, it is one of the biggest storms I've seen in all my years here but I've put up with these long, dark, cold, godforsaken winters all this time, and I haven't jumped off that blasted dock yet!" she said in disgust.

"Me neither," Gladys added. "But don't think it hasn't entered our minds."

The men looked shocked. "You mean you have actually thought about it before?" Dan asked. He did a visual survey of the women in the room. Most of them solemnly nodded their heads. There was silence for a moment as the men absorbed this revelation.

"Well, yes, of course, we've all thought about it. But haven't any of us ever done any more than think of it!" Betty finally retorted. "Besides, if we jumped, then who'd be here to keep all you fellas from jumping?"

Laughter lightened the pall of seriousness that had been apparent in the group.

"We're all nuts to stay here in this frozen meat country, I guess," Jim said.

"Is she really beautiful?" Mike's wife asked.

"I wouldn't say she was all that pretty. Would you, Mike?" Jim answered.

"Naw, sorta plain looking really. All except them legs! She's got pretty ones of them," Mike said. "But no prettier than yours used to be," he added, after his wife jabbed him with an elbow.

"You men! You'd think none of us girls had legs!" Betty sputtered. She stamped one of her own plump ones, pretending to be angry.

"Well, if'n you do, none of us has ever seen 'em. All we see is a bunch a squaws in hip waders most of the time. I lived here longer'n the rest a yous, and I swear in all that time I never seen a lady in a dress in this damned town!" a waterlogged old fisherman said.

"If you didn't stink like rotten fish all the time, you might've had a better chance!" Betty retorted with a grin.

The crowd in the cafe began to disperse as morning approached. Sunday mornings were usually quiet and this one would also be. Jim walked the block to the clinic and spent the morning watching for signs of returning life in the woman.

Thirty years came and went. One cool late October morning a ten-year-old girl sat on a stool, chin resting on cupped hands, watching an older woman roll out cookie dough.

"Grandma?"

"Um?"

"Is it really true how Grandpa said you and him met?"

"You and he," she corrected.

"You and he. Is it true that he found you up to your ass in mud and pulled you out?"

The grandmother looked shocked. "You shouldn't talk like that," she scolded.

"But that's 'xactly what he said," the child protested. "He said you hated it here so bad you tried to drown yourself in the mud. But he saved you."

Francine smiled. "Yes, honey, that's exactly what happened. He rescued me. The old fart made me fall in love with him, and here I've been ever since."

The little girl snickered at the description of her beloved grandfather.

"Have you ever been sorry, Grandma?"

Francine pushed a stray lock of graying hair away from her face with the back of her hand and looked at the serious-eyed child. "Well, they say 'home is where your heart is.' From that first day at the clinic when I opened my eyes and saw him sitting there holding my hand, mine has been here with your gramps. I've had no regrets."

The child stared dreamy-eyed as she listened to her grandmother's version of the romantic tale. She roused when the older woman said, "Now, how about helping me cut this dough into Halloween witches and goblins?"

Forever Lost

Anchorage Daily News, Saturday, September 6

FAMILY OF FOUR MISSING,
INTENSIVE AIR SEARCH UNDERWAY

Four members of the Elliott Lloyd family left Friday morning on a flight to Seattle.   Relatives became concerned and notified authorities when they did not arrive at their destination.   The last known transmission from the single engine Cessna was received shortly before noon in Juneau when Lloyd, a veteran pilot, radioed his location and asked for weather updates. No further word has been received, and it is assumed the plane went down somewhere between Juneau and Prince Rupert, B.C., possibly on one of the many uninhabited islands. A number of search planes have been dispatched in an all out effort to locate the missing plane and any survivors. Lloyd, chief executive officer for Lloyd and Smythe Investment Company, with his wife and two children, planned to spend this holiday weekend with relatives in Seattle.

Energy ran high as Elliott herded his family from the station wagon, parked near the runway of the tiny airport, into the single engine Cessna. Luggage enough to last two weeks was loaded in back, even though they would just be gone three days. Peggy, his wife, helped secure their two children's seat belts, then buckled herself into the seat next to his. He noticed the heightened color in her cheeks, excitement for the trip clearly visible on her face. It reminded him of the way she'd looked in that moment on their recent wedding anniversary when he'd presented her with the gold locket, which now hung around her neck. Inside it was a small picture of the four of them, snuggled close together and smiling.

"I'm looking forward to this trip," she sighed. "It seems like it's been such a long time since we've had a chance to get away with just the family." Her full time job as assistant to the president of the local bank and the hours of volunteer work she put in for various organizations kept her terribly busy. With her added obligations as mother of a precocious seven-year old son and an energetic thirteen-year old daughter, she was hardly left with time to think.

"I know," Elliott said, reaching over to pat her hand. "This will be a wonderful weekend. It'll be nice to see your family again." He was really thinking how great it was going to be to take the plane up. It had been a couple of months since he'd found time to indulge his passion. He particularly enjoyed flying this time of year—the long days of summer were disappearing at the rate of six minutes a day until now, near the autumnal equinox, the daylight hours nearly matched the dark ones—making it seem more like those he knew as a child growing up in Montana.

After his customary equipment check, he was satisfied that everything was functioning correctly. He taxied to the end of the runway, and when cleared to take off, they lifted into the air, banking over the small radio tower as they headed across the mountains. They soon picked up the coastline and followed it south.

When they approached Juneau, Elliott radioed the local tower. "This is Mike Bravo Charlie niner-four-three. Request weather information, Prince Rupert."

"Radio tower, Juneau. Prince Rupert reporting overcast skies, ceiling 25,000 feet, visibility thirty miles. Potential for patches of fog," came the response.

"Thank you. Over and out." He felt relaxed and cast a glance at his wife. He watched her, thinking how beautiful she was and how contented she seemed as she gazed out her window at the capitol city clinging to the steep mountainside below. Both kids were already napping in the back, snuggled into their pillows like a pair of puppies with full stomachs.

Elliott knew the route well. He had flown it often, not always all the way to Seattle, but frequently enough that he was familiar with the landmarks. Every so often he looked out his side window, keeping the mainland in view to the east, as they flew over a myriad of obscure, uninhabited islands. He scrutinized the passing scene below, watching for specific points that served to guide him—a small village tucked away at the end of an inlet, a peculiarly shaped island, or an open barge lumbering its way along the inside passage, indicating the location of the main channel.

He glanced at his family again, all asleep now, lulled by the constant, monotonous thrum of the engine. The afternoon sun warmed the aircraft, making him feel relaxed. He'd flown for about an hour when he saw the cloudbank ahead. As he approached, he realized it was an area of thick fog surrounding the remote islands scattered beneath it. He turned towards the mainland, hoping to avoid it, but it was moving rapidly and before he could clear it, the plane was suddenly completely enveloped. He was instantly alert, leaning forward trying to see through the window, but it was impossible. He could not tell exactly where, or how far above the land they were.

He dropped down hoping to come out from beneath the mist giving him enough visibility to be able to guide the plane out of the soup. But the lower he brought the plane, the thicker it seemed to be. He felt panic for the first time in his flying career. He tried to gauge where they were. Now that he'd changed course, he wasn't sure if they had reached the mainland, were over open water, or were still flying above one of the many uninhabited islands.

Not until the impact did he know. The jolt was unbelievable. Stunned, he stared straight ahead trying to understand why he couldn't see. Then it slowly dawned on him that blood was pumping from his forehead and cascading down his face. He swiped an arm across his eyes to remove some of the stickiness. The plane was at a forty-five degree angle, the nose buried in earth. He could tell he had broken ribs and was shaken, but other than the pain in his left side and the surface wound on his forehead he seemed to be okay.

He looked to see how his family had withstood the crash, and what he saw made his heart stop. Peggy's neck was twisted and her head hung at a skewed angle, her eyes half open, her mouth slack. She was dead. Panic seized him as he struggled to unbuckle his seat belt. He finally freed himself and twisted around to the back seat to reach his children. A deep gash had broken through the skull leaving his son's brain exposed and his small body covered in blood. Elliott knew he, too, was dead. Tears gushed from his eyes, blinding him afresh, as he reached across his son's dead body to lift the head of his daughter where it slumped against her chest. It lifted limply, as if there was not a single bone in her neck. His entire family gone in an instant! A cry of anguish rose in his throat, rending the silence of the cockpit, until the unearthly sound deafened his own hearing.

He forced the door open and staggered to the ground, his knees buckling the instant his feet touched. He crumpled into a tight ball, the top of his head pressed against the earth, both hands clasped behind his neck, and rocked back and forth, wailing into his own bruised chest.

Anchorage Daily News, Monday, September 8

SEARCH CONTINUES FOR MISSING FAMILY

Search efforts have increased in Southeastern Alaska for a prominent businessman and his family, missing since Friday.

Additional planes have joined the effort to locate the plane of Elliott Lloyd or any survivors. A spokesperson states there have not been any clues or signs of the single engine Cessna carrying the family to Seattle for a weekend visit. Family and friends remain hopeful, citing Lloyd's skill as a pilot and knowledge of the area.

Moving slowly and mechanically as if in a nightmare, Elliott ripped apart one of the pillowcases and bound his ribcage. He packed the emergency survival gear and some foodstuffs into his army knapsack and prepared to walk for help. He had no idea where he was, only that he was somewhere in Southeastern Alaska. Whether he'd crashed on the mainland, on one of the inhabited islands, or on one of the small, more remote and unpopulated ones, he could not tell.

Then, overwhelmed by the extreme sense of loss, he leaned against the cold metal of the wreckage, clutching the gold locket from his wife's neck tightly in his hand, and wept anew. The image of the broken bodies of his family—now shrouded together under a green woolen army blanket where he'd placed them in the rear seat of the plane—were vivid in his minds-eye, and he begged their forgiveness. "I should have turned back as soon as I saw the cloud bank," he sobbed. "It's my fault, all my fault."

Finally, with reluctance, he pulled himself away and began walking. Tall trees hid from his view any telltale signs that would indicate a coastline or promontory, either of which might aid in his rescue. He could only guess which way to go, and in the end he chose to go towards the east, somehow sensing he was on an island somewhere along the inside passage, which meant the mainland lay in that direction.

Simple breathing made his lungs hurt. He walked slowly, stopping often to lower the pack from his back, hoping to ease the pain and burning in his ribs. His head ached where it had been gashed, and he began to notice other discomforts that had been overlooked in the beginning. He dug around in the pack, found the painkillers, and swallowed some tablets without water.

He knew he'd only traveled a couple of miles, at most, by the time the shadows became long and the sun began to sink below the horizon at his back. He spotted a growth of old pine nearby that stood grouped together forming a semi-circle. The ground was uneven and covered with sharp needles but provided some protection and he decided against building a fire. He was too sore to lie down, so he got as comfortable as he could leaning against the trunk of one of the larger trees. After forcing down one of the sandwiches he'd saved from the ice chest, he wrapped himself in an army blanket and tried to sleep.

The dark hours seemed to drag by. He shifted positions frequently, hoping to get some much-needed rest, knowing his bruised body would need strength to walk for help in the morning. The throbbing in his ribs kept him from sleeping, and he was aware of night sounds. As an experienced outdoorsman, none of these sounds were strange to him. Instead he found them somewhat comforting—all except the eerie unidentifiable sounds he heard in that coldest hour just before dawn, sitting huddled with his knees drawn into his body attempting to stay warm. From somewhere on the mountain above him he thought he heard a woman weeping. It drifted with the shift of the winds, seeming to come from different directions, leaving him feeling unnerved and anxious. Finally, he reasoned it must only be the wind creating friction between trees somewhere in the forest.

As soon as there was enough light to see clearly, he gathered his things and began to walk again, heading into the rising sun. All that day and through the next, Elliott slowly worked his way toward the east, stopping frequently to rest. He ate little, slept even less.

Anchorage Daily News, Wednesday, September 10

SEARCHERS LOSING HOPE OF FINDING SURVIVORS

Hope is diminishing as day five search efforts for missing family end. More than two dozen planes have joined in an attempt to locate the Elliott Lloyd family, missing since last Friday. Most of the coastal region of Southeastern Alaska has been combed as well as many of the larger islands. Residents of towns in the region have been interviewed in hopes someone may have seen or heard the single engine Cessna after it cleared Juneau. Nothing has been turned up. Weather forecasts indicate an approaching front, which rescuers fear may hamper efforts as early as tomorrow.

At noon on the fourth day, Elliott sat on a grassy knoll forcing himself to eat. The soreness in his ribs was still sharply painful, the wound on his head felt feverish as if infection had set in, and his exposed skin was sunburned and itched where mosquitoes had feasted. His motions were methodical and automatic as he chewed slowly, without tasting the salty pungency of the moose jerky. He was so lost in thought as he gazed morosely into the happy faces of his family, smiling out at him from the gold locket, that at first he didn't hear the airplane engine.

When it finally registered in his mind, he stood too quickly. His head begin to reel, and he had to sit again until it cleared. Excitedly he looked for the plane, finally spotting it in the north, still a long way off. It flew towards the east, banked back towards the south, coming closer to where he sat, but long before it came close enough for him to attempt to signal, it turned back towards the north and slowly disappeared out of sight.

"At least they are looking for me," he thought, feeling a twinge of hope, even through his disappointment. "Maybe tomorrow."

That night he again found protection in a stand of trees and made his camp. He'd discovered a position on his right side where he could lie down, making it easier to sleep. Each passing night seemed to grow colder than the ones before and, even though he'd built a fire he shivered under the army blanket. As on previous nights, he was awakened again by unfamiliar sounds, and he lay awake for a long time listening intently, passing time by trying to identify each one—howls of a coyote pack, tree branches swaying in the wind, a night bird calling its mate—all familiar.

He must have drifted off to sleep, for when he opened

his eyes, dim images of his surroundings were visible in the pre-dawn light. He moved stiffly, stretching to loosen up his shoulders and neck muscles, then clamped his eyes shut, wincing at the stab of pain from his broken ribs. When the ache subsided, he opened his eyes and what he saw gave him a start. Perched above him on a limb of the tree, and staring at him through coal black eyes, was a Tlingit native, strangely dressed in an ancient costume—tanned moose-hide tunic and trousers, and white ceremonial-beaded moccasins on his feet. The man did not move nor blink, but seemed to be silently watching Elliott, a scowl clearly visible on his face.

"I crashed my plane. I was beginning to think help would never come," Elliott began, after recovering from the initial shock of seeing this strange sight. He struggled to stand. With a sense of relief, he began to gather his things and fold his blanket, wondering how long this visitor had been there.

"Thank goodness you found me," he said, thinking it strange the man had not identified himself. He was also surprised that he'd not heard this visitor's arrival. When there was no reply, Elliott looked up into the tree, but the man was not there. He couldn't see the Indian anywhere. Bewildered, he called, "Wait for me. I've been injured and I'm moving a little slow." But there was no sign of the stranger anywhere.

Feeling frustrated and angry, Elliott decided the man may not speak English but had surely realized that help was needed, so had hurried off to get some. For most of the day he stayed close to the area, reasoning that his rescuers would expect him to stay put, making it easier for them to find him.

The weather turned foul and a cold drizzle set in, but

he continued to wait. He waited the entire day, but with nightfall he realized he'd been mistaken in his assumptions and prepared to spend another night in the same camp. He built a fire again, choked down the contents of a can of chili, and crawled under his blanket.

The next morning, he decided to change the general direction of his path, heading toward the north where he'd seen the search aircraft a couple of days before. Continuing to stay out in the open, yet near the forested ridge, he traversed several miles over the next two days. The dreary dank weather showed no sign of letting up, keeping him constantly wet. But he struggled on in a slow march, listening for planes, although he knew none would be flying with the weather socked in as it was.

Anchorage Daily News, Saturday, September 13

SEARCH EFFORTS TEMPORARILY SUSPENDED

Search efforts for the Elliott Lloyd family and their single-engine Cessna, missing for one week in Southeastern Alaska, have been suspended until weather clears. The front that passed through Wednesday night has made visibility nearly impossible in the area where the plane is assumed to have gone down. Hopes of finding survivors diminish as friends and family keep vigil.

The terrain subtly shifted from the higher ground,

where he'd spent the past several days within the relative protection of trees, to open tundra, harder to navigate. He struggled ahead for several hours, floundering and falling frequently as he worked for footing on the uneven, soggy ground. By mid-afternoon he collapsed, sank to his knees, then flopped onto his back, spread-eagle amidst tufts of lichen—exhausted, stupefied, and disoriented.

He was still in this position—face up in the rain, totally wet, shivering violently, thirsty, and hungry—when he roused from his stupor. He forced his eyes open and looked around trying to get his bearings. Then, to his surprise, he saw a man a few feet away with a heavy black beard, standing, arms akimbo, observing him, the corners of his mouth drawn down in a look of apparent disapproval. This man was nothing like the quaintly dressed Tlingit. He was a giant man, nearly seven-feet tall, wearing a red-and-black plaid shirt, jeans, lumberjack boots, and a red stocking cap. His presence was overpowering and unnerving, and at first Elliott couldn't speak. "The Indian must have sent you," he finally said. The big man didn't move.

"I'll get my things," he said, turning to find his knapsack, grateful help had finally arrived. But when he slung the bag over his shoulder and prepared to leave, the giant, too, had disappeared.

Confused and angry, he struggled to his feet and turned in every direction looking for the black-bearded man. All he saw was a distant hillock where a thicket of closely-knit willows had grown. He staggered to his feet and drunkenly floundered his way to them. He knew he needed to get out of his wet clothing and boots. But when he dug in his knapsack for dry ones, he moaned in disbelief. It had fallen open and everything inside was soaked—his one change of clothes, blanket, food, and his entire supply of matches.

In wild desperation he searched his pockets for the gold locket, fearful the picture of his family, too, had gotten wet and was ruined. But when he opened it and found the treasured photo still intact—four smiling faces looking happy and unconcerned—he clutched it to his chest, sank to his knees, and cried until there were no tears left. Such horrible pain and guilt he'd never felt before. "Forgive me. Forgive me," he repeated over and over, wanting it desperately, yet never allowing himself to feel forgiven.

Finally, after he was completely spent, and having no other choice, he pulled the soggy woolen blanket from the pack and crawled under it to endure another long, lonely night in the wild, the locket clamped tightly in his fist.

Anchorage Daily News, Monday, September 15

SEARCH FOR MISSING FAMILY CALLED OFF

Search efforts to locate the family of Elliott Lloyd, missing since September 5, has been cancelled. It is assumed that the single engine Cessna on a flight to Seattle crashed somewhere in the waters off Southeastern Alaska and that there are no survivors. A memorial service will be held on Friday, says a family spokesperson. The location and time will be announced later this week.

Elliott lay still, staring into the canopy of willows. That he'd slept for a full night without moving was clear to him from the stiffness in his back. He was very disoriented and spent several minutes trying to make out the strange shapes hovering over him. At first his eyes focused only on the slender boughs of the wispy trees bending near his face. He realized the sun had briefly broken through the clouds. Then, as his distant vision cleared, he was startled to again see faces peering down at him—one the Tlingit, the other the giant lumberjack—both with bland looks of disinterest in their eyes.

For several long, angry moments he looked at them. "Help me," he demanded. His voice cracked, allowing no more than a whimper to pass his lips. "Why won't you help me?" Neither of the two strangers appeared to have heard him, nor did they speak. They gave him one more empty look, and as before, they swiftly began to move away.

He jerked upright and struggled to free himself of the tangle of bush. On hands and knees he cleared the thicket. He watched as they seemed to almost skim across the tundra. He was suddenly in a rage. "I'm going to turn you into the authorities as soon as I get back to town. There's a law of common decency that requires you to help me." He tried to yell, but the sound of his voice came back to him pathetic and squeaky. He struggled with his pack, shoving in his blanket as he attempted to follow them. Ignoring his pain and weakness, he pursued them, a strange demented energy urging him on.

At times he was so fatigued he forgot everything except the need to keep putting one foot in front of the other.

Seldom taking his eyes from the uneven ground, he stumbled blindly on, trying to maintain some balance, yet falling often. He knew his energy was waning quickly and he was tempted to not get up again. But a stronger sense of injustice forced him on. He dragged himself erect, searched the horizon until he located the two men, then staggered ahead. At times it seemed they had stopped to wait for him, but each time as he'd draw nearer they'd move off again. A new surge of anger would propel him onwards—reeling, disoriented, and uncontrolled like an inebriated sailor making his way down a back alley grappling at light poles as he drunkenly galloped from one to the next.

Towards late afternoon, the Indian and the giant stopped and turned to face him. Panting, he forced himself into a dizzy trot, straining to reach them. They stood rigidly waiting until he was almost near enough to see their eyes. But before he reached them, they each raised a hand in farewell and disappeared over the edge of a hill.

By the time he reached the crest, the two were nowhere to be seen. But what he did see was welcomed. He'd reached the edge of a cliff overlooking a broad sandy beach, and in the distance he could see other islands dotting across an inlet of ocean.

He clamored down the face of the cliff that stood between him and the smooth sand below, slipping and sliding hysterically in his rush. When he reached the beach he shed his pack, dropped to his knees and began to weep. He gave himself up to the complete fatigue that overtook him, curling into the fetal position before passing out; all that was left of him was a pitiful human ball of unconsciousness, lost on a remote deserted coast.

It was pitch black, except for a few stars shining through openings in the clouds, when he was rudely dragged back to consciousness. An icy wave washed across him making him gasp and struggle for breath. He was totally wet. Memories of his loss, still too fresh and painful to have become fully ingrained in his mind, left him feeling completely disoriented. He listened for identifying sounds around him and heard only the monotonous rhythm of the ocean as waves rose and fell. He remembered then and knew the tide was coming in. He was too weak to move. "This is where I die," he thought. The idea comforted him and he let the ocean wash over him again and again.

Perhaps it was just a dream that roused him from his lethargy. Perhaps it was his innate will to live. But he suddenly felt compelled to seek higher ground, as if his wife and children were calling him. He fumbled in the darkness until he located his pack and dragged himself away from the rising water. He slowly shrugged off his wet clothes and wrapped the blanket around his freezing body.

Then, with a strange sense that his family was with him, he had an overpowering need to clutch them near. He dug into the pockets of his jeans, searching for his only means of holding them—the locket. It was not there. On his knees now, his burning frostbitten toes digging into the sand, he frantically dug through the knapsack, tossing everything out in a feverish search. The gold locket was missing.

Grief poured from him in keening wails, the disconsolate sound mingling with and becoming lost in the roar of ocean waves. His tears, hot and salty, flowed from sunken eyes and coursed down his unshaven face. The slowly mending ribs screamed with the pain of his racking sobs. At long last, his emotions spent, an all-encompassing weariness overtook him. Rolling from his knees to his side, he looked into the moonless sky. "Please, let me die tonight," he prayed, his last thought before he lapsed into a dreamless sleep.

When he woke for yet another day, the rain had ceased and the sun was high overhead, blasting directly into his face. He was feverish, his teeth chattered from the cold air, his entire body ached, his throat was parched, his toes were blue and numb. His vision was dim, his muscles weak and sluggish. He no longer felt thirst nor had any pangs of hunger. That he had survived the night surprised him and for a moment he thought there might still be a chance he'd be rescued.

But when he forced himself to focus, he remembered it had been days—maybe ten—since the accident. He knew that by now the search would have been called off. "I'm a dead man," he thought. "I only hope it comes soon."

He found the idea of death appealing; with it would come forgiveness for his negligence in not turning back when the fog blinded him, causing the demise of his entire family—death, his ultimate reprieve. A smile flickered across his dry, swollen lips as he closed his eyes one last time.

The bundle of human flesh, swathed only in a filthy green army blanket, lay unmoving upon the beach. No sign of life remained. But, as the sun passed across the top edge of the cliff, a flicker of light caught the attention of a passing bush plane.

Anchorage Daily News, Tuesday, September 16

ELLIOTT LLOYD FOUND ALIVE

A bush plane, attracted by what appeared to be a flashing distress signal, located the missing pilot on a remote uninhabited island in Southeastern Alaska yesterday. Lloyd, his family, and their single engine Cessna have been the focus of an extensive air search. Peggy Elliott and their two children were killed in the crash. The rescue plane had not participated in the search. Its pilot—a hunting guide—along with a companion, were on a scouting mission looking for mountain goats on another island. He said Lloyd was alive but in poor condition when they reached him. Lloyd reported that two men, one a Tlingit native, the other apparently a lumber worker, repeatedly approached him throughout the ordeal but refused to offer aid. He intends to press charges against the two men. Lloyd is recovering in a Juneau hospital.

Elliott resisted hands roughly rousing him. He felt his body being moved.

"This must be the guy from the family they've been searching for," he heard a male voice say.

"Yes. I heard they called it off yesterday. Figured after this length of time they'd never find them. I'm amazed he's still alive," the other man said. The two men stripped off his soggy blanket and Elliott groaned.

"Me too, but I'd say just barely alive. Look at him."

"Man, look at his feet. He's going to lose those toes, is my guess." They wrapped him in a warm blanket.

"We better get some liquid in him," the first man said and pried Elliott's mouth open. He could feel hot coffee being forced down his throat.

He strained to open his eyes and when he did get them open he seemed unable to focus on his rescuers. Instead, what he saw were two shadowy, but familiar figures, standing at the top of the cliff. He weakly rose up on an elbow and pointed. "That's them," he rasped.

The two rescuers looked to where Elliot had indicated. "What do you mean?" one asked.

"There. Those two guys. Wouldn't help me. Just looked and walked away." His elbow gave way, and he slumped back into the blanket.

"There isn't anyone there," one of the men said, giving his companion a quizzical look.

Elliott continued to look at the cliff. "They're right there," he said again, pointing urgently. "They left me to die. I'll get even with them. That's a promise."

The rescuers carefully carried the stricken man and loaded him into the plane. One of them gathered his scattered articles and stuffed them back into his pack and loaded it also. The pilot made one more search of the area and was preparing to climb back into the plane when a flash of light from up on the cliff caught his attention. He saw a bright object spin through the air and slide down the slope as if it had been thrown from the ledge. Curious, he climbed the bank and retrieved it.

"This must be what caused the flash of sunlight that

caught our attention," he said, handing a gold locket to his companion. "He must have dropped it in just the right spot for the sun to make a mirror of it. Lucky, I'd say."

His companion looked at the small object in his hand. "Strange. I suppose it could be, but I wonder what made it fall down the cliff just now."

There was no answer for the mystery. The plane roared to life, taxied along the beach and lifted into the air, turning towards Juneau.

Anchorage Daily News, Thursday, September 18

CAUSE OF CRASH UNDER INVESTIGATION

Authorities are investigating the cause of the crash of a single-engine Cessna, which cost the lives of a woman and two children. The plane, piloted by Elliott Lloyd, husband and father of the victims, disappeared September 5, and was the focus of an intensive air search for two weeks before Lloyd was found alive earlier this week. Questioning has revealed possible pilot negligence in the case. Family members of Mrs. Lloyd have pressed wrongful death charges against Lloyd, citing carelessness as the reason for the tragic accident. When asked in an interview for a response to this news, Lloyd said, "Some things are worse than death. It would have been better if I'd died with my family than to have to live with these regrets for the rest of my life. I wish I'd never been found."

Moose

Jo Massey

I can see you're a stranger here, ma'am. Sure, everybody knows him. I think he just went out on a wrecker call and won't be back for a while. We all just call him Moose, you know. Why don't you sit down here and join me for a cup of coffee while you wait? I'll tell you about him.

His full name, as you said it, is Walter Arthur Norman Thomas. That makes his initials W.A.N.T.. I always thought it was sort of ironic, like one of those fate things, how his life hasn't ever turned out quite like he hoped—left him wanting, so to speak. Probably him being thirteen pounds at birth, and born breach to boot, had something to do with his ma's naming him for every male alive in his family at the time. She never wanted to have another kid after that ordeal. And she didn't. She figured him and his older sister were enough. Yep, thirteen pounds at birth and he never stopped growing until he gained another three hundred pounds and reached six foot five.

He owns his own garage now, you know, and by

most accounts he's a pretty fair mechanic. But a lousy businessman. I'll bet if everyone who owed him money paid up on the same day, he could take that trip to Hawaii, plus have plenty left over to buy a new trailer house when he got home. He owns that old trailer he lives in now, back of his shop—bought if off a guy that lived here for a dozen years or so and who one day just up and said he'd had enough. He asked Moose, 'Do you want it or not for what I owe for you fixing up my truck? I gotta get the hell outa this godforsaken country.'

It sounded like a good deal to Moose, so he said, 'sure,' and pulled it over from where the guy had it parked out by that bridge south of town. Up till then, he'd lived in a one-room apartment in the basement at his sister's noisy house. She had six kids by the time he moved out.

The sign says WALTER'S GARAGE, but like I said, nobody that knows him ever calls him Walter. He can always tell if it's a stranger in town in need of mechaniking because they come in asking if he's Walter. "Well, yeah," he'll drawl, kind of suspiciously, and ask why they want to know. Then they'll tell him about their Winnebago that's making a funny noise, or it'll be some guy on foot, telling him about the station wagon with his old lady and a passel of kids broke down back along the road somewhere or maybe somebody who wants him to weld up the tongue on their trailer, filled with all their junk, so they can go back to Texas or Oklahoma or wherever it was they came from in the first place.

Hey, Betty, bring this lady a cup of coffee, will you?

Say, are you having car trouble? Is that why you're asking for him? No? Oh, that's good. You're answering his ad? You hear that, Betty? Guess he must have finally decided to get himself a bookkeeper. About time, I'd say.

"That's the truth. He really could use someone to help keep things straight," Betty said. "Not meaning to be nosey, Miss, but did you come with that Japanese tour group? No? Oh, I thought maybe you were one of them."

Yeah, that Moose. He's a real character. I'd say practically his whole life has been just one mishap after another. Most of 'em are pretty funny to us that knows him well. We rib him a lot and most times he takes it good-naturedly.

Like, for instance, there was one time clear back in the first grade. Our teacher, Mrs. O'Grady, let us keep all kinds of little critters in cages so we could learn how to take care of them. One was a little hamster we named Peewee. He was a real tame little guy and at recess she'd let us play with him.

Well, this one day, Mrs. O'Grady was sick or something so we had a substitute teacher. I don't remember her name, but she was real young and pretty and this was her very first day ever teaching. Well, at recess we were all clambering to get to hold Peewee and she let Moose hold him first. Then one of the other boys wanted a turn but Moose wasn't quite done holding him yet. So they got in a little tussle and the other kid started grabbing and Moose started squeezing and the next thing anybody knew, Peewee's eyeballs were popped out on his fat little cheeks and there was blood running out his nose and everywhere.

One of the little girls screamed and when Moose saw Peewee's condition there in his hands, he got scared and threw it against the wall, which left a big splat of blood right there.

Then each of the rest of us boys, curious you know, had to pick up the poor mangled little Peewee to see for ourselves. In turn we'd get all squeamish and we'd fling it around some more until we'd just splattered blood and guts all over the place. Mary Jo Hendricks got so sick she vomited and that made some of the other girls vomit, and it was one of the goriest scenes you could ever imagine. Moose felt real bad, of course, and his ma made him buy the class another gerbil. But Peewee-Ella just didn't seem to fill the void. I heard that poor teacher gave up teaching and became an accountant or something.

You need a warm-up on your coffee there, ma'am? Hey, Betty, how about bringing that pot over here?

Then there was the time—I think it must've been along about the fourth or fifth grade—Moose had a trap line up on the creek behind their old home place. He was trapping for beaver or muskrats or whatever else he could catch. Talked about how he wanted a beaver hide to make himself an Indian drum. He'd seen about how to do it in some boy's magazine.

Well, this one day, see, he goes out to check his traps. Takes his big sister with him—the one who ended up with the six kids—and what does he have in a trap but a wolverine. Now, I don't know if you know anything about wolverines or not, but next to a brown she-bear, they're probably the meanest critter in all the north woods. Fortunately, this one here was kinda small, but still very much alive and not a darn bit happy about what was going on.

Well, of course, they didn't have a gun or anything like that with them, because his old man wouldn't let a young kid like him carry a weapon. So they decided they had to kill that nasty-tempered old hellcat with a big rock. But the problem was to keep from getting torn up themselves.

So he talked his sister into taking off her rabbit fur coat so he could use it as a shield. I bet you can guess what happened to that coat! He got close enough and threw it over the critter and started bashing the poor thing in the head with a big rock. Finally it went limp so he thought he had it killed and he released it from the trap and wrapped it up in her coat, that's pretty much ruined by now anyhow.

So then they start out for home and pretty soon that dead wolverine starts moving around so they have to set it down and beat on the poor thing some more. And they go on for a ways and it starts wiggling again. So they kill it again. In a few more minutes the same thing happened and they had to stop and kill it again. The darn thing didn't seem to be smart enough to just go ahead, give it up and die in earnest.

Well, finally their ma saw them coming a mile off and got their dad from whatever he was doing to go see what they're up to and she tells him, for God's sake, not to let them in the house with whatever it is they have. He got the .22 and went out to meet them and put that ugly, bloody beast out of its misery. Then he handed them a shovel and made them go out in the woods and bury it.

Of course, a wolverine don't smell quite as bad as those skunks they have in the lower 48, but they don't smell none too pretty either and that musky scent sort of rubbed off on Moose. I remember he got to take a couple of days off from school until some of the stink wore off. His sister was pretty mad about her coat for a long time.

Oh, hiya, Jim. Want to join this nice lady and me?

She's waiting for Moose. I was just telling her about him. You remember how he came by his name, don't you Jim?

"You bet I remember that story. That day sure stands out in my mind, like it was only yesterday. Good morning, Betty. Bring another cup of coffee over here, please?"

Well, you probably think he got the name from his size. Lots of other folks do, too, but that isn't it. It happened along about the time we were boys in junior high school, like the eighth grade or so. He was already a strapping big kid by then and probably clumsier than ever. You know how boys are around that age—all feet and legs and dangly arms and an Adam's apple twice as big as their scrawny necks have room to hold.

"Don't forget the pimples," Jim chimed in. "Him with that rusty colored complexion, he had plenty of them."

That's a fact! Well, his best friend at the time was this old black lab named Fame. There again, that name was probably one of his ma's fancy ideas, knowing how weird she was about names. So one day him and Fame were out in the woods just goofing around like a guy and his dog will do, and he looked up and saw this big old bull moose standing right there at the edge of the willows looking at them. Not looking at him exactly, but staring with a sort of nervous, walleyed-look at Fame.

Then, without warning that moose came charging out of the willows with his head down, shaking his antlers, big as plow blades, and he laid into that dog.

Well sir, that big dumb kid, without thinking a blooming second about his own hide, went roaring over to where that moose had his dog down and started whaling away with his fists and feet, punching and kicking that mangy old moose—mad enough to kill with his bare hands.

So, old Mr. Moose turned his head around and stared right in the eyes of this kid that he could wipe out with just one little swipe of his antlers, and he kind of blinked in surprise. Then he turned and ran—I mean literally ran as fast as he could—off into the brush.

That scared kid came running home to tell us the story and, at first, we thought maybe he was making it all up. That is until we saw the blood all over Fame. We all went back to the spot where it happened and sure enough, there they were—big moose tracks all around the place, mixed up with his and Fame's.

That's the day folks started giving him a lot more respect, and from that day to this, nobody but strangers ever call him anything but Moose. See, that's how I knew you weren't from around here.

That Fame sure was a good old dog. He finally died of old age.

"Oh, don't forget to tell her about that motorcycle deal," Jim said. "That's a really funny story."

You're right. I don't remember now for sure if the Harley incident was before or after the night he borrowed his dad's brand spanking new Ford station wagon and took a bunch of us boys riding. He had permission, of course—wasn't the kind of guy to do anything that wasn't right up front. He picked us all up and we went cruising town and ended up driving out the highway to see what was happening at Shorty's.

Of course, we weren't any of us old enough to go into

the bars, but somehow we'd gotten hold of some beer anyway. So we were just out there messing around, downing a few beers, and he decided to see really how fast that car could go. Thought he'd give us all a little thrill, too, going down that long hill just out past the cemetery there.

Anyway, we went flying down off that hill and were nearly airborne by the time we hit the bottom. Blam! That was a real neck snapper. Remember, they didn't make springs back then like the kind of shock absorbers we have nowadays. Well, after that happened, he decided we'd probably had all the riding around we needed for one night so we headed for home. He never could hold his liquor too good and he got sick on the way. Puked in the car, right there on his dad's new upholstery. That didn't do anything to make the rest of us feel better.

"I sorta remember up-chucking that night myself," Jim chuckled.

Well, so, anyway, the next day, Moose, still looking pretty green around the gills and this time on foot, came by my house and told me how his dad woke him up, mad as hell, yelling about what the blankety-blank did you do to my brand new car? Seems all four tires were flat as pancakes and there was that puke all over the seats! We didn't go riding together again for a long time after that.

Yeah, now that I think of it, the Harley was after that. It's the only time I can remember Moose ever did anything kind of sneaky. He bought this old—oh, probably about a 1931—red Harley off some guy that'd ridden it all the way up the Alcan, if you can imagine that. It was pretty beat up but the price was right. Fifty bucks as I recall. Seems he'd saved that much money up doing odd jobs for the principal and some of the teachers at school. His old man was still mad about the car incident and he wouldn't have been any too pleased with his buying a motorcycle, so Moose stashed it over behind someone's outhouse. Then he'd take it out riding every chance he got.

Well, this one fine spring day, along about the middle of July, he went out riding up where that old picnic area used to be before Exxon bought the land and built that big building there. A bunch of girls, probably from a summer camp, were playing volleyball and sitting around drinking lemonade, all wearing shorts, of course. And Moose's eyes got to wandering over the scenery, so to speak, and he forgot to watch where he was going. He completely missed seeing the ledge he went flying over until it was too late.

He told me later that at the time he somehow was thinking that if he jumped off the motorcycle he'd just land on the road and the motorcycle would go on without him. Well, of course, if you know anything about physics, you know that didn't work. He went flying down the bank, crashed through a tree standing there and landed head first in the creek.

He thought he was dead for sure, would drown even if all the internal bleeding didn't do it. Then, he said he heard this calm voice somewhere there in his head telling him he really owed it to himself to try to get out of the situation. So he pushed with his hands and sure enough, his nose cleared the water so he could breath. He looked up and there was a guy running down the bank, with a chain and everything, ready to pull him and his bike back topside.

His goal of getting the girl's attention was certainly realized, because they were all standing up there gawking over the edge at him. When they saw he was all right, they went back to their game and that was the last he ever saw of them. Oh, he had lots of scrapes and bruises but that was all. His pride was what was the most injured. He sure was a tough bugger, that one.

You sure you wouldn't like a piece of pie or something to go with your coffee? They make the pies up fresh every day. The apple's my favorite. Hey, Betty, bring us three pieces of that apple pie, will you? It'll be my treat.

"You want that pie heated?" Betty asked. "Okay, it'll just take a couple of minutes."

"Put a scoop of vanilla ice cream on mine," Jim said.

Moose was never too lucky at love, neither. All the girls in school adored him in a big brother, friendly sort of way. Sure, any one of them that didn't have a real boyfriend at the time would be glad to go with him to a dance or party, but just as friends. There was one he had a pretty big crush on for a while—Carol Ann. I wonder what ever happened to her. I'll have to ask someone one of these days just to satisfy my own curiosity.

She was one of the cheerleaders the year Moose won the state wrestling championship. Boy, I remember that year well. All us guys went out for wrestling. Before every meet we'd go without eating or drinking for a day or so, then get in the sweat box to lose even more pounds so we could weigh in light enough to be matched to a littler guy. Of course, the other team had been doing the same thing, so we probably ended up wrestling the same guy we would've anyway, but nobody ever seemed to think about that.

I remember one time being so constipated from

dehydration it nearly cracked the porcelain when it hit the bowl! Oops, sorry ma'am. Guess I got a little carried away there for a second. But, Moose didn't have to go through all that. The bigger the better if you're in the heavyweight division.

He was a good wrestler. You'd see his broad ass sprawled out with some guy squirming under him pinned to the mat. I think we took state that year. Carol Ann would give him a big hug after he'd won a match and he'd grin and drip sweat all over her. Then she'd go off for a soda with Tom or Bill or someone else and he'd just stand there looking after her like a lost puppy.

Then, along came that Vietnam thing. We were all at the right age to be drafted so we figured we might as well join the Navy early on. Most of us went right to the heart of the action, but by some strange fluke or act of fate, they sent Moose off to Hawaii, of all places. Guess they thought he'd be a good bodyguard for the Captain of the Pacific fleet because of his size.

So, there he was, just driving the brass around paradise. Well, one day he made a little mistake with one of the big boys in the back seat. When he turned to go to the base, he accidentally went the wrong way on a big one-way four-lane highway. Suddenly he looked up and noticed the red light change and then a wall of cars coming right for them. So he thought real fast and threw that big car into reverse and tore down the road backwards about sixty miles an hour.

He likes to tell about looking in the rearview mirror and watching that officer swooping around in the back seat like some turpentined cat. He laughs that big old barrel laugh of his every time he tells that story.

For a while there it looked like all the practice he'd had driving his dad's cars, most of which were junk when he finished with them, had finally paid off, saving the Captain's life and all. But that old goat wasn't impressed the least little bit, because as soon as he could, he had Moose reassigned to other duty somewhere clear across the base. Everything turned out okay in the end though, once they found out he could work on cars better than he could drive them.

"Here's that pie," Betty said. "I hope I'm not being rude, Miss, by asking, but if you aren't Japanese, you must be Korean then? Ah, yes, I thought so. I always have such a hard time telling the difference."

Go ahead and sink your teeth into a bite of that pie and tell me what you think. Isn't it about the best you ever tasted?

"Ummm, Betty, you might have outdone yourself on this one," Jim said.

"Thanks. Oh, don't forget to tell her the story about Moose's solo flight. I love that one.," Betty chuckled.

Oh yeah. That is a good one. Well, you see, after he got out of the service and came home, he decided to take up flying. Somehow, he got his hands on an old Taylor Craft that needed new fabric—that means the wings needed to be recovered. He spent all winter stretching and stitching and finally got it done.

One day, after he had the plane all put back together, it was my sorry luck to be the one he invited to go out to the airport with him on a late Sunday afternoon to look at it. He talked me into getting up in the passenger seat so I could admire his handiwork on the interior. Well, there wasn't anyone around so he got the bright idea of starting it up and just taxiing it up and down the runway a few times. You understand, he'd just been reading about flying, hadn't actually starting taking any real lessons yet.

As I recall, it was a perfectly calm day, but suddenly, out of nowhere, a gust of wind blew up. Next thing I knew the whole plane was off the ground. I looked over at him and I could see he was trying to figure out what to do. He had clocked in a lot of hours on the back of heavy equipment, so he shoved in on the throttle, just like he would to shut down a dozer. Only thing was, on this airplane, you were supposed to pull the throttle back to stop. So here we were lifting off the ground in earnest and by now he seemed to be getting a little excited and started grabbing knobs and turning paler by the second. Finally, thinking fast like he rarely does, he just reached up and turned off the magnetos, figuring, like he told me afterward, that if you don't know what to do it's best to do nothing.

Now, if you've ever wondered what a plane does if the engine stops running, I'm here to tell you that it just falls straight out of the air wherever it happens to be. That new chain link fence around the airport made a regular shish-ka-bob out of that flying machine, with the two of us bobbing around up there looking for all the world like a couple of all-day suckers on sticks. Which, I promise, is about how I felt—just like a big sucker, and not the sweet kind. Then some drunk guy walks by—he was staggering and talked with a slur—and he looks up at us and says, 'What happened here? Did this thing just fall out of the sky, or what?'

Me and Moose laughed until we cried, and it helped keep the whole incident from seeming so serious. So much for his one and only solo flight. Mine too!

I see it didn't take you long to finish off your pie? I told you it was really good.

Well, I've been sitting here telling you all the funny stories about good old Moose, but, like everyone else, there's a few that's been sad. Like, as I mentioned before, his luck with women hasn't been the best. But, he finally had a romance of sorts.

It was with Bill's wife, Leota, after Bill died. She was kind of a crazy thing for a while when she was going through the 'change.' Went off with some guy who worked for Exxon. I always thought her running off like that might have had something to do with Bill's killing himself, but I could be wrong. I heard she'd already decided to come back home before she got the news about Bill.

Anyway, for a long time after the funeral, we'd see Leota and Moose together, and we kind of hoped it would work out for both of them. She's not a bad woman, really—a sharp dresser, keeps herself nice. Loves to dance. I suppose that's one reason it didn't work out for the two of them. Moose is pretty awkward on the dance floor—lives up to his nickname—looks for all the world like one of them barrel-chested critters lurching around on long legs. I sort of felt sorry for him after she left. He gets pretty lonesome sometimes, I think.

I'm ready for another warm up. What about you, ma'am? Jim?

But I'd have to say my favorite story about Moose is

the one from just last spring at Bill's funeral. Since you're not from around here I don't suppose you know about that. It's been all the talk around here ever since it happened.

Bill was probably Moose's best friend and the poor guy took his suicide harder than anyone. I think in a way he blames himself for not going with Bill that night—like maybe if he had of it would of changed the way things turned out. We all felt terrible about it, of course.

Well, before the funeral all us pallbearers had imbibed a little more than we should have. I'll be the first to admit it. But we were trying to jack up our courage to face the ordeal. So none of us were really at our best, isn't that right, Jim? It was terrible—right there during spring break-up when everything's so messy and sloppy anyway.

It was a pretty sorry mess, even before the hearse buried itself in the mud. Anyway, when that happened there wasn't anything else to do but carry the casket by hand the whole way up the hill through the cemetery. Every blessed step was sticky as gumbo and before we knew what was happening, Moose slipped and fell into the grave. That knocked the rest of us off balance and we fumbled around and dropped the casket in on top of him. Christ-a-mighty, you should have heard the ruckus he put up. Of course, at the time it wasn't at all funny to him. Could have been downright serious, in fact.

We couldn't get the casket out of the hole to free him and had to send to town for a backhoe to go all the way out there to rescue him. By then it had struck the rest of us just how ridiculous it all was, and we just about busted a gut trying to keep a straight face. Even the preacher had to snicker.

The only people who didn't laugh were Bill's mother and his widow and, of course, Moose. Poor old Moose still doesn't seem to be able to see anything funny about the whole thing—turns kind of pale when anyone even mentions it.

Speaking of Moose, he should be coming along here anytime now. I've never known him to be late for Thursday's blue plate special. Betty's meatloaf and mashed potatoes are about as good as it gets.

You know, I've been sitting here thinking about what you said about answering his ad. I don't remember seeing any ad in the paper. Do you Betty? Oh, you have a copy there? Oh, no wonder—it's the Seattle paper.

Ummm. Well, well, well, I'll be hornswoggled. Hey, Jim, Betty. You need to look at this! It says, *Bride wanted immediately. I'm not fussy. Must be willing to move to Alaska. Ask for William Arthur Norman Thomas.* Can you believe that?

Well, it's sure been a pleasure talking to you, Miss. I hate to run, but I suddenly remembered something I've got to do. Thanks for the coffee, Betty. See you around, Jim.

"Hurry back, you hear?" Betty said. "Oh, look, Miss, here's Moose driving up now."

Dolly's Revenge

Jo Massey

Except for the hum of the teakettle on the wood cook stove, the cabin was quiet. Dolly looked up from her paperback when the cuckoo clock sprang from its nest to announce the hour. Hank Shanklin's radio talk show came on at seven o-clock Sunday nights and she rose from the only easy chair in the sparsely furnished room, snapped on the Motorola, and dialed to the Anchorage station.

She checked the pot on the back of the stove, ladled the remains of the week's stew into a bowl and walked with it to the door and looked out.

It had been dark for four hours already, but after twenty-eight years in Alaska, she no longer thought the dark days of winter to be in the least unusual. The weather was clear. She guessed the temperature to be about ten degrees below zero and glanced at the large-faced thermometer attached to the gatepost in the yard to confirm her guess. The clear, crisp air made perfect conditions for an aurora borealis, she thought, as she returned to her chair. Hank's opening remarks, intending to incite a lively discussion, asked the listeners if they thought dog mushers were animal abusers. The responses were varied and heated.

Dolly wondered if Henry would come home tonight. He'd gone to Anchorage three days ago under the pretext of having to buy a case of oil for the old pickup. She saw right through him. He hadn't changed the oil himself for years. She guessed he must think she was too stupid to know it was Fur Rendezvous weekend. Last year, when they had gone together, he'd left her sitting in the truck for hours while he whooped it up in a bar with a wild bunch of lowlifes. That was their quarrel that put her in the hospital. She hoped that this year he'd stay in town long enough to sober up before coming home.

A flash of headlights beamed through the window, making a slow arch across the far wall of the main room of the cabin. Her heart sank. That would be him making the turn into the lane. She steeled herself, determined, once again, that she would not do anything to upset him.

She heard the clatter of the engine of his old work truck as it pulled in front of the house, then his footsteps on the porch. Uneven, clumsy stamping told her that, as she already suspected, he was drunk. The door swung open. Brutus, the huge, burly, half-Malamute-half-wolf, ran in first, rushed to his bowl and began noisily chewing dry dog food. Henry blinked and stared jerkily around, apparently bewildered by the light of the open bulb hanging in the center of the room over the heavy oak table. His arms swung loosely by his side, and he stumbled to the table, slumping into a chair. He spied her in the ugly green chair pretending to be reading.

"Whershhh my shupper, woman?" he demanded.

She ignored him.

"I whan shumm goddamn shupper! I ain't had nuthin' ta eat all goddamn day. I'm shhtarvin. Git your fat ashh up n' fix me shumpon ta eat! And shut off that goddamn noise."

Dolly turned the radio off, set her book aside and stood looking at him. "All right, I'll make you some eggs and toast," she said, her own eyes narrowing as she attempted to avoid his bloodshot ones.

"I don't wan' no goddamn eggs and toast," he mimicked. "I wan' a shhteak. Fix me a shhteak! Now, dammit. Or elshh you'll wishh you had."

She knew what "or else" meant. The cast had come off her arm just two weeks ago for the last "or else." She started toward the back room to get a moose steak from cold storage, but he grabbed her and swung her to face him. She grimaced with the pain that ran down the still-healing arm. Brutus lifted his head from his food bowl and growled at her.

"Don't get shhmart with me, woman!" he snarled, and slapped her hard with an open hand across the cheek. The force snapped her head to one side. She turned back to face him.

"Don't hit me again," she said in a slow, even voice.

"I'll hitcha any time I whhana," he said.

"You ever hit me again, it'll be the last time," she hissed through clenched teeth.

He doubled his fist and struck her hard, full in the face. She staggered backward clutching the edge of the cabinet to keep from falling.

He let go of her arm and used both fists to beat her, landing punch after punch in her face and abdomen. She tried to run from him into the small bedroom, but he grabbed her around the waist and swung her back into the room. He yanked a handful of her hair and pulled her head back until it seemed he would break her neck. Brutus, excited by the fracas, joined the fray. He growled meanly, bared his teeth and bit at her leg. His teeth scraped her calf but did not penetrate the flesh.

"Like I shhay, I'll hitcha any time I whanna n' ain't nothin' you can do 'bout it." He shoved her away, hurtling her to the floor. "Me'n Brutus, here, are goddamn shhick a your attitude."

She crept to the far corner and pulled herself into a sitting position, knees pulled tight against her aching bosom. Her right eye was beginning to swell already. She was unable to cry.

Henry crossed to the cabinet where a sink should have been. "I'll jushhh drink my shupper, then." He fumbled around behind a bucket in the base of the cabinet, and finally pulled out a bottle of whiskey. He'd never bothered to put plumbing in the house—thought a galvanized pail to hold fresh water and an old chipped wash pan, with a hole draining into a slop bucket, were just fine.

Dolly didn't raise her head, but she knew from the long moment of silence that he was drinking deep. The only sounds were the tea kettle sizzling innocently on the cook stove, his stagger to the table, a chair scraping against the hardwood floor, a heavy thud as he dropped his large loose-jointed frame into it, the slam of the bottle onto the scarred surface. Brutus gave one more low, throaty growl, and then sank to the floor under the table at Henry's feet. Then there was a moment of silence—probably him taking another swig, she thought—before she heard the soft sound of a fleshy head falling onto oak.

Dolly sat hugging her knees, breathing shallowly, waiting for his stupor to deepen. She was going to do it. She had promised herself over and over again one day she was going to do it. Always before, she had forgiven him after his repentant pleadings in the days that followed one of these bouts. But this was the last and final time. He would never touch her again.

She listened to his breathing. When it finally grew deep and his snoring loud, she knew he would be unconscious for hours. Only then did she shakily stand to her feet, pushing her hands against the wall for support. She felt her way across the room, all the while facing the hulk collapsed at the table. The dog lifted his head from the floor, giving her a surly, green-eyed glare, curling one side of his lip, but he let her pass. She slipped past the row of open shelves where the dishes were stored and backed around the corner into the bedroom beyond. She pulled aside the curtain separating the two rooms so she could keep an eye on the drunken man.

The tarnished mirror hanging over the washbasin revealed what she already knew. Her right eye was nearly swollen shut. A deep purple bruise on her cheek was beginning to show. Blood, now dried, formed a single line from the edge of her puffy lip to her chin. The trail led to a large stain drying on her gray sweatshirt.

She was not a pretty woman on the best of days. She

had never imagined herself as anything but plain. Even as a child her face had been too large, too round, too bony, too boring. Her best facial feature was her porcelain blue eyes, now barely visible. Her eyebrows had turned a deeper shade of blondish gray. In her youth, they had been snowy white blond, so much so that they made her face, all except the two round red dabs on her cheeks, look pale. Her hair had been that same startling blond. It was hard to tell the difference between that white blond of then from the white gray of now.

She pulled off the sweatshirt and examined her body for more bruises. A red knuckle-shaped mark on the left breast glared at her. Even her breasts were plain. They were not at all like the ones of the women in the Playboy magazines Henry sometimes used to taunt her with. Hers were basically just functional—the kind her hardy German forebears had used to nurse robust babies. Hers had never suckled a child. That was the one thing she was thankful for in her ill-begotten union with Henry—there had been no children

She saw two bluish marks growing on her abdomen. The trunk of her body had thickened in the last few years since she turned fifty, but her belly was still flat. It didn't have the softly sensual rounded shape of a mother. Her arms were the large-boned, heavily muscled arms of the homesteader woman she was. The newly mended one bore fresh purple fingerprints.

She poured cold water from the pitcher into the washbasin and dampened a thin worn-out washcloth. She gingerly bathed her face as she gazed steadily into the remaining un-swollen eye. This time I'm going to do it, she vowed again. She felt calm in her resolve.

She walked to the one battered bureau in the small bedroom and pulled open a drawer to get a fresh sweatshirt. The young couple in the faded wedding picture in the cheap gilt frame smiled out at her. She looked into the bright happy eyes of the round-faced, rosy-cheeked bride. This was the closest to pretty she'd ever been. The groom would have been rather handsome in a dark rugged way if it were not for the two large flappy ears extending from either side of his bearded face. She hadn't minded his ears being so large. She'd actually felt lucky to find a strong husband with his spirit for adventure and fun. But he'd taken her from family and friends in Illinois within days of the wedding to travel north in search of fortune in this frozen land.

If she'd only known then what she knew now, she thought. She'd probably have married that homely little Jimmie Tatum from the neighboring farm instead, had lots of freckle-faced children, gone to PTA meetings, raised a big garden, maybe even been a member of the Presbyterian Church.

She picked up the picture with a sigh and turned it face down on the bureau. The innocent smiling faces in it made her horribly sad.

A sudden sound from the other room made her jump, and she moved to where she could get a full view of Henry. The hand grasping the bottle had relaxed and fallen to the table. Aware of the dog's cruel eyes following her moves, she walked into the room and stood over the silent man.

His face was pressed nearly flat-nosed onto the table; his head tilted just enough to allow his sour-mash breath to escape. His left earlobe flopped against the wooden surface. Curly thick dark hair stood up at odd angles around his head from where his stocking cap had been removed and tossed aside. There was no sign of graying yet. His right hand, thick fingers extended, lay flat near the edge of the table.

Dolly studied him several long moments, then deliberately went to the cold back porch. She returned with a hammer and some sixteen-penny nails. Brutus watched her suspiciously from his spot on the floor.

"It's okay," she told him softly, and he lay his head back down onto one of Henry's feet.

The first nail drove easily through the ear lobe with three or four blows. There was no response from the stupefied man. She bent the nail in on itself. Dolly was glad for her years of handyman experience. If any repairs ever got done on the place, she'd been the one to do them. She drove the second spike through the fleshy muscle between the thumb and forefinger of the outstretched right hand and bent it down. The damaged nerves made the fingers twitch for a few seconds before they fell lax again.

His face showed no sign of consciousness. The dog caught the scent of fresh blood and growled, but detecting no movement from his master, he lay still. Dolly slid the bottle away from the left hand and the curled fingers went limp. One more short series of blows with her hammer left the abusive man completely vulnerable.

She returned the hammer to its place on the cold porch and came back with a dusty leather suitcase. Without a glance at the still form nailed to the table, she walked through the curtained doorway to the bedroom and began to pack her meager possessions—underwear, socks, sweatshirts, pajamas, jeans. From the makeshift closet, she pulled a few print blouses from hangers, a gray flannel skirt, white cardigan, and a pair of black wool slacks.

In a corner of the room was a stack of milk crates piled on their sides forming cubbyholes—a sort of chest of drawers—that held her clothes. She pulled out some sweaters. One, pink cashmere with hand-stitched bead trim, was preserved in heavy plastic. She drew it from its wrapping and ran her coarse hand across its softness. She laid the pink sweater and black wool slacks aside on the bed and folded and packed everything else into the suitcase.

Fingering the few items in her cheap wooden jewelry case, she searched for anything she valued. She lifted the short string of pearls she'd worn on her wedding day, a cross on a silver chain, her mother's cloisonné broach, and wrapped them in a silk scarf. Then she tucked the treasures into a side pocket of the suitcase.

Have I missed anything, she wondered, surveying the room. The moneybox! She raised the old braided rug by the bed, revealing a loose floorboard. She lifted it and pulled out a homemade wooden box with a brass hasp and tiny gold padlock. She rose and went to the one small window in the room, pulled back the faded yellow curtain and removed a piece of loose chinking, drawing a small key from its familiar hiding place. She glanced into the main room to be sure Henry had not stirred before she opened the box.

A manila envelope, soft and worn with age, held her precious little savings. There was no need to count it. She knew exactly how much was there. It had taken years of ingenuity, stealth, and self control, to put away the almost three thousand dollars. Most of it was in small bills—ones, fives, tens, and a few twenties. She slipped some of the bills into her black plastic purse and buried the rest under her clothes before zipping the suitcase shut.

She was ready. Only the wait was left. Many years of pain, both physical and mental, had brought her to this moment. A little more waiting wouldn't hurt. It might be pleasant, actually, to have a few quiet hours to anticipate her imminent freedom.

She went to the kitchen. Henry's breathing was the deep and jagged kind brought on by alcohol-induced coma. A small stream of drool had run from his slightly parted lips and pooled on the table. His lips were chapped, his cheeks brown and cracked from too much time in the snow with Brutus and his precious dog team. He looked so innocent and vulnerable that she almost felt sorry for him.

Dolly reached onto the highest shelf of the open cupboard and carefully lifted down one of the seldom-used china teacups and a matching saucer. She was going to have a cup of tea. Henry never allowed her to drink tea in his presence. "It's a sissy woman thing. It looks stupid on a big old broad like you," he'd said.

The other fragile cup of the set had been broken when he slapped it from her hand so many years ago. She selected a tea bag from its hiding place in an empty baking soda can and poured hot water over it, then went to sit in the green chair to think over her plan.

She was surprised at her own calmness in the face of the major step she was about to take. What would happen to her, she wondered. Anything would be better than this life.

Dolly finished her tea, returned to the bedroom and slipped out of her clothes. She gave her body a sponge bath and slid naked into the bed. It was nine o'clock. She was tired, bruised and sore, and needed to sleep.

Several hours later a sound woke her. It was Brutus scratching at the door to be let out. She looked at the clock. Five-fifteen. It would still be dark for another six hours. She let the dog out and checked on Henry. He had not moved. His breathing was now the more steady rhythm of normal sleep, and she knew he would be coming around soon. She had not stoked the fire nor added any wood since just before Henry's return home last night. The house was cold.

Dolly quickly dressed in the traveling clothes she had laid out. She noticed the bruises on her trunk turning deeper black and quickly pulled the sweater on. She had always loved the pink sweater but had only worn it a couple of times in the six or seven years she'd owned it. There hadn't been much reason for her to dress up. She stepped into the wool slacks and pulled them up over her flattish masculine-shaped hips. In younger days, she had been concerned over her lack of curves, but over the years she had learned to care little for her looks.

The Malamute wanted back in, and when she opened the door she felt the bite of cold air on her feet. The temperature had continued to drop during the night and it was now thirty below zero. The surly animal stalked past her. Henry began to stir when Brutus nuzzled his leg before lying down again under the table.

She hurriedly pulled on socks and laced her boots.

She knew the time for the final act of this drama was arriving.

Dolly brought her purse, the suitcase, and her parka from the bedroom and placed them in full view next to the green chair. She lifted the double barrel shotgun from its place on the hooks over the door. Then she sat in the chair facing the disabled man with the gun resting across her knees. She wanted to be able to see his eyes when he opened them.

Henry's breathing changed, so she knew he was waking up. He stirred and coughed. His elbows moved, his back lifted, his shoulders raised. He mumbled. His shoulders heaved again, and she could hear his breathing speeding up.

"What's going on? Something's wrong with me," he said, his voice rising in fear. "Oh, God. I've had me a stroke or something."

He struggled to pull his hand free and lift his head. "God, oh, God. Something terrible's wrong. Dolly? You there? Come quick. I can't move." His voice was shrill now and his upper body was heaving and jerking. "Dolly, wake up. Help me."

Brutus had sprung from under the table, glared at her, somehow knowing she was responsible, and began pawing at Henry's leg.

"That you, boy?" Henry said. "Go get Dolly."

The dog ran to her barking and snarling. She continued to sit in silence.

Henry uncrossed his feet, placed his weight on them and tried to stand. The chair slid backward and crashed to the floor. He stood but could not pull his body free from the table, and he slumped to his knees on the floor. "What the hell?"

He was fully awake now. Then he saw the nail

driven through the web of his hand and the dried bloodstain on the table. "Sonofabitch! What have you done to me?" he yelled.

He let his eyes rove the room looking for her. At last he saw her and his gaze came to rest on the shotgun in Dolly's lap, then slowly up to her bruised and swollen face.

"Oh, God!" he moaned. "Dolly, please don't," he said, his voice pleading.

She didn't move or answer.

"Damn. I did it again, didn't I? Oh, Doll Baby, I'm so sorry. I didn't know what I was doing. You know I wouldn't hurt you for anything. Honest. Not unless I was drunk. Or you did something to make me really mad." There was a pause. "What did you do this time to make me hurt you?"

She ignored his question. "I nailed you down so you can't ever hurt me again," she finally replied in an even tone.

He began to whine. "Okay, dammit, you win. I promise I'll stop drinking. I'll really do it this time. Just please take these goddamn nails out. I can't move."

His bloodshot eyes searched her face for a flicker of conciliation but found none. "I'll go get them pills that'll make me sick if I even look at a drink. I'll see a shrink. Anything. Just please turn me loose. Don't do this," he pleaded.

She didn't move, and he seemed to know he would never convince her of his good intentions. He took another tack, apparently trying to shame her.

"At least when I hurt you, its the booze doing it. You done this to me stone sober. You are a heartless and cruel woman. Only a really evil person would do something so horrible to a helpless man."

She sat immobile, staring at him with her hands resting on the gun.

"I told you to never hit me again," she repeated, and her voice was sad. She raised the shotgun to her shoulder.

Henry began to weep. "Oh, God, please don't," he wailed. "I'll change. I promise. Please don't kill me."

He looked pleadingly at her, sincere tears of regret streaming from his eyes. He saw the long cold steel of the barrel and her cold-as-steel blue eyes at the other end.

"Dolly, please. I know I'm a no-good bum. You've every right to be mad. I'll change. Just give me one more chance. Please don't kill me." He looked pitifully at her, but her expression showed no sign of compassion.

She clicked the safety off, adjusted the gun to her shoulder and squeezed the trigger. The blast reverberated around the cabin, and then all was still. Dolly lowered the gun slightly, not taking her eyes from the man. Then satisfied, she lowered it to the floor, stood, put on her parka, and picked up her suitcase and purse.

"Oh, God! You shot my dog! You shot Brutus!" Henry's voice was shrill, hurt, angry. "Why'd you go and shoot my dog? He ain't ever done nothing to you."

Dolly walked past him to the door, opened it wide and stepped through it. "Just wait. I'll get you good for this!" Henry screeched.

She disappeared as silently as an apparition into the blanket of icy February fog that surged into the room.

"Come back here! Please, let's talk this over." A sound of contrition crept into his voice. "Come back. It's freezing in here. If you don't shut the door and build up the fire, I'll freeze to death!"

His pleas dimmed and wavered in the arctic air until she could no longer hear them as she walked toward the pickup. She started the engine, backed away from the cabin, and drove down the lane to the main road.

Jo Massey

Adult Education

Jo Massey

The room was noisy with pre-class chatter in excited anticipation of the first meeting. It was obvious most of the people knew each other, were in fact fellow employees of a well-known hotel chain. They had come straight from work and were still wearing identical blazers bearing the gold company insignia. Their employer had paid for them to attend this public speaking class to help improve their proficiency in dealing with the prestigious convention customers.

A young Inupiat woman, dressed in blue jeans and T-shirt, entered and glanced about uneasily. Several of the group looked at her with slight scowls, then ignoring her, turned back to their conversation. She timidly slid past a group of men laughing and talking animatedly about some incident they had shared at work that day.

Talk stopped as she passed, then one whispered, "What's she doing here?"

Another replied, "Beats me. Maybe she's in the wrong

place. Probably supposed to be in a basket-weaving class or something." The others laughed.

The girl pretended not to hear and took an inconspicuous seat in the back corner of the room just as the professor arrived. He checked the clock on the wall, and when it was 7:30 he began outlining the syllabus of the class.

He was five minutes into his presentation when a large, rather uncouth woman entered the back of the room and pushed her way to the front. Her oversized bag bounced across a couple of empty desks, then clunked a stuffy-looking gentleman in the head. She didn't seem to notice.

A hush fell over the room as everyone gaped at this unusual looking woman. Her bleached-blond hair had been teased into a bouffant and was bound with a hot pink sports band. Her matching hot pink velour blouse fit loosely over a portly frame and reached mid-thigh, where it stretched over form-fitting black tights stuffed into battered shoes with three-inch heels.

"S'cuse me," she said to the professor. "Sorry I'm late, and for the first class, too. Darned impolite of me. My apologies." She looked at him demurely from beneath blue-painted eyelids with, what one would suppose was meant to be, a charming smile.

"That's okay," he said, looking a little irritated as he waited for her to get settled.

The room became quiet as the class watched her force her stubby body into the confines of the school desk. She shoved her satchel under it, glanced up with another smile at the professor, and folded her hands on the desk. Then, as if she just remembered why she was here, she began rummaging in her bag again, the only sound in the room, and eventually came up with a notebook and pen. She seemed pleased and settled back, ready to learn.

The professor pulled himself and the rest of the class back from the unexpected distraction. "I thought it might be a good idea in this first class if we took a little time getting acquainted with one another. I would like for each of you to choose someone to work with. Each of the partners should take about ten minutes to interview the other person, and when everyone has finished, we will take turns introducing one another."

There was a buzz in the room as people made a mad scramble to find someone other than the strange woman to work with. Only the shy young Inupiat girl in the back was left without a partner. The girl glanced around the room with uncertainty, a look verging on panic in her eyes

"Well, honey, I guess it's you 'n' me," Hot Pink said as she squeezed herself into the seat opposite the girl and scooted closer.

The girl swallowed hard, forced a meek smile, and with resignation slipped back into her seat.

"This'll be easy as spittin' in the wind," the woman said. "How's 'bout I go first since you look kinda scared about it all? You jus write down what I say, and then you can read it back to 'em when they call on you, okay?"

The girl nodded bleakly and positioned her pen over her notebook, waiting.

"Well, ain't you gonna ask me somethin'?"

In a thin, wavering voice the girl gulped, then asked, "What is your name?"

"Oh, that's easy. My name is Elsie Marie Pritchard." She stuck out her pudgy hand for the girl to shake but the girl didn't notice because she was looking at her note pad. "Hmmm," she mused and continued, "I used to be Elsie Marie Baggs until I married Mr. Pritchard. I was only too glad to get rid of that stupid old name," she giggled. "Baggs. Can you just imagine all the stupid jokes I had to put up with?"

The girl nodded, then scribbled in her notebook and waited, apparently trying to think of another question. Elsie looked at her, and finally said, "Well, I'll jest keep on talkin' and you can write down anythin' you think's 'portant, okay?" She looked at the girl and saw her nod.

"Well, now, let's see, where was I? Oh, yeah, I was speakin' of Mr. Pritchard. He was sure one good-lookin' boy when we was young. We got married right as soon as I finished the tenth grade. He didn't finish high school neither, but he had a good job workin' for his uncle Johnny in the oil patch. My folks was real proud a him and always told me how lucky I was to make such a good catch." She paused to be sure the girl was taking notes.

"I started havin' babies right away. Eight of 'em altogether. Five girls and three boys. Thank the good Lord they're all alive 'n well. Boy, howdy, don't you know I was one busy little gal with all them younguns? And us a movin' all the time, from one oil patch to another. Timmy, that's the oldest boy, is a big shot in some investment company in San Francisco. He don't get to make it home too much anymore. His daddy misses him mor'n any of the other kids. They was thick as pea soup when he was growin up—always goin' fishin', or throwin' balls, or somethin'.

"Marybelle, the oldest girl, is married to a banker, and they moved off down to Seattle. She calls sometimes, but her husband thinks he's lots better'n us and don't like for her and her little girls to come visitin'. I guess I yearn to see her 'bout the most. I used to say she was my little straw flower. Yeller hair and eyes blue as the sky.

"Ruthie come next. She's a little bit slow so she stays close to home. A nice girl — just kinda simple-minded if'n you know what I mean. But she learned how to cook and cooks real good, too. Ain't nobody can beat her cornbread and beans! You gettin' all this down?" Elsie looked sharply at her partner to find the girl's black eyes fixed intently on her face. The girl looked swiftly away and began to scribble on the pad.

"Say, what's your name?" Elsie asked abruptly. "I like to know who I'm talkin' to." She reached across the space between them and patted the girl on the arm.

"Brenda Ninishka," the girl replied and smiled shyly. "I like your story. Go on."

"Brrrennnda," Elsie rolled the name across her tongue. "Nice name. I wish I'd a thought about that name for one of my gals. I'll bet you're real smart, too, ain't you?"

Brenda blushed and looked down at her notebook before answering. "Well, I do have a 3.8 average so far. This is my second year here."

"See, I could tell. I'm a real good judge a people. So, I was telling you 'bout my kids. Well now, after Ruthie came little John. We've always called him little John since that's his daddy's name. They're lots alike in some ways. Little John quit school in the tenth grade like me, and started mechanikin'. There ain't an engine built that little John can't fix. He's got hisself a cute little wife—kinda reminds me a you in a way, except she's some older. They got two darlin' little boys and one a them's named John too. We call him baby John, but I reckon we'll have to quit that real soon. He jus started kindigarden and I don't guess he'll 'preciate bein' called 'Baby'." She laughed out loud and clapped her chubby hands together. Several people looked their way, but she didn't notice. She picked up the chronology from where she'd left off.

"Then Betty Lou came along. She was the squallin'est baby I ever saw. Was just plain mad all the time. Grew up with a chip on her shoulder the size of a breadbox. A real feisty little gal. She's a senior in college now and makin' life miserable for someone else for a change. I bet she don't ever find a man to put up with her temper. Whew! I could really tell ya some stories 'bout her! If I'd a known how she was gonna be, I probably would'na ever had any more kids, but the good Lord knew the next one was gonna be a gem.

"Patty Ann. Purty as a pi'ture from the day she popped out! And sweet as apple pie. Just can't do enough to please us or her teachers or friends. Everybody just loves her. Straight A's all the way through school. Even got a scholarship for college next year. Going right here so she can stay at home and help us out." Elsie's face beamed with pride.

Brenda was listening with interest and diligently taking notes.

"Well, we're down to the two younguns. Bobby comes next. He's kinda roly-poly like me." Elsie giggled easily, poking fun at her own figure. "He's the best darned tackle on the high school football team this year. He ain't the smartest kid, but he's got lotsa friends and a good attitude.

"And finally, the youngest is Susie. She's still a little girl with pigtails and freckles and she'd rather play GI Joe with the boys than play Barbies with the girls. Too early to tell what she's gonna turn out like." Elsie looked at Brenda. "Maybe she'll be smart like you, honey."

Brenda glanced up from her notebook, a pleased look on her face. "Thank you," she said. There was a pause. Elsie sat with hands folded and appeared to have finished.

"But Mrs. Pritchard," Brenda began.

"Now, honey, call me Elsie, please, like you and me was friends."

"All right, thank you." Brenda smiled at her appreciatively. "The main question I have, Elsie, is why are you taking this class?"

Elsie leaned back in her seat and stared for a long moment at some invisible spot on the ceiling. "Well, it's like this, ya see." She looked back at Brenda. "My darlin' Mr. Pritchard has jest 'bout used up his gorgeous body, workin' so hard for me and the kids and he ain't gonna be able to keep on doin' it much longer. And ever' time I go out to see 'bout a job so's I can help 'im out, I get told I don't have nuthin' to offer. Ain't got a college education, got no work experience, seems like I don't really amount to much. So I says to myself, I gotta go get an education so's I'll be worth somethin'. All the years I watched my younguns march off to school and become successful gents and ladies, I have to tell ya, in my heart I was kinda jealous. Not green-eyed-evil jealous, of course. Just wished I'd had the same chance." She sighed, releasing her breath slowly through her nostrils.

"My dear man and those sweet children a mine all said, 'Momma, now's your turn to go to school.' I darn near cried when they pushed me out the door tonight, all wavin' and smilin'." Elsie rubbed her pink velour sleeve across her misting eyes. "I'm just so gosh-darn proud to be here!"

There was a brief pause as Elsie regained her composure. "Okay, now, honey, tell me all about yourself."

Ten minutes later when the class resumed, the professor asked for a volunteer to be first to introduce their partner. Elsie was the first one with her hand in the air. He looked past her and chose someone else to come to the front. Each time another person concluded their introduction her hand was again raised but passed over. Finally her vigorously waving arm, swathed in hot pink and jiggling charm bracelets, could not be ignored, and she was allowed to take her place at the front of the class. The other students fidgeted in their seats, looking somewhere other than at this woman that they perceived as ignorant and uncouth. But finally curiosity got the best of them and they watched her from lowered eyelids. Elsie was not bothered by their apparent discomfort.

"Hi, there. My name is Elsie Marie Pritchard. And that there little gal in the back is my new friend, Brenda Nini..." She stopped to peer at her notes.

"Brenda Nini-shaka? I forgot how you say it," she said, looking at the girl.

"Ninishka," Brenda prompted in a near whisper.

"Ni-nish-ka," Elsie repeated. "And she's from Unalakleet over on the Bering Sea. She's here going to school. Must be a real smart little cookie, 'cuz the Alaska Native

Association gave her a scholarship and everything." The woman beamed at the girl with a look of mother's pride.

"Now, Brenda here is kinda shy. I noticed that right off. But it's cuz she's never been to a big city like this before in all her seventeen years. That, and the fact that those Inupiat people don't seem to talk too much anyway. My husband's been around some of those remote villages a lot on his oil field job and he told me they have other ways of communicatin'. Anyway, the poor child's sorta an orphan, I guess you could say. Her daddy got killed on a whale hunt when she was just a little thing. Then her momma died about four years ago. Just got sick one day and died a week later. That left Brenda here and her two little brothers all alone. They went to live with their daddy's brother that's got ten kids—all younger than her. I guess, to hear it, that's one crowded house! So, she's real lucky to get to come here to live for a while. Course, bein' a student and all, she can't afford to live in a very big place. So she's just rentin' a little room above the North Star Laundry over on C Street."

Elsie looked at her audience and noticed that she now had everyone's attention.

"And, you know what makes this little gal so unusual?" Elsie leaned across the lectern in a conspiratorial gesture, looking straight into the eyes of each person in the room and waiting for some response. Several people turned to look at the young Inupiat woman. Color rose in Brenda's cheeks and she lowered her eyes.

"What is it that you find so unusual about her?" the professor finally asked.

"Well, she's come to get a teacher's certificate so's she

can go back to her village to teach the kids there—her brothers and cousins and all the rest. Ain't too many kids these days that finally get away from home that ever wants to go back. Sure not to live, anyway."

Three months later, snow was falling the evening of the final class, two weeks before Christmas. Elsie and Brenda arrived together and were greeted warmly as they entered the room.

To allow time for refreshments after class in celebration of the end of the term and the upcoming holidays, that night's assignment was for each student to give just a short talk. Each was to tell briefly what he or she felt they had gained by taking the class. Most of the talks were generic in tone about how the class had helped the student to be more effective in their individual jobs.

Brenda waited until only she and Elsie were left to speak. During the course of the class she had surprised the others by giving speeches that were not only well thought out and well prepared, but were also skillfully delivered. Her timidity seemed to disappear once she was behind the lectern.

"The most important thing I have gained from this class has not been the public speaking, although, of course, that has been very valuable." She looked comfortable and confident as she smiled at her audience. "If I had not taken this class I'd still be living over the laundry and feeling lost and alone much of the time, for I would not have had the opportunity of meeting Elsie Pritchard." She looked pointedly at her friend.

"Elsie and her family have made room for me not only in their home, but in their hearts as well. I feel like I am cared for as if I were one of their children. I want to publicly thank her for her kindness and generosity to me." The applause was heartfelt and warm as she returned to her seat.

Everyone looked at Elsie expectantly, eager to hear her final speech. Over the weeks they had learned that even though her talks rarely followed the expected structure, they would always be creative, entertaining, and colorful.

"Remember the first night of class and little Brenda here told you the reason I was takin' this class? She said it was so's I could get educated enough to get a job so's I could help my dear Mr. Pritchard support all of us. Remember?" She paused to make sure everyone was with her.

"Well, then, I'm just so right-down proud to announce to all a you that you're lookin' at a workin' gal! Yessiree, that's right. And it's all thanks to that new, sorta 'dopted daughter a mine, sittin' right there." She gestured with an arm smothered in gaudy costume bracelets towards Brenda.

"Yep, she spoke a good word for me to get interviewed with one of the big-wigs over at the Native Association and they practically hired me on the spot. Can you believe it?" Pride showed on her face, as she made eye contact with her classmates.

"But, I'll just bet you all can't never guess what my job's goin' to be. Try!"

There were guesses ranging from 'receptionist' to 'janitor.'

"Nope. Nope. Nope," she said, giggling at their missed answers.

"I'm to be their new spokesman, er, rather that's spokes*woman*. I get to travel out to all the villages all over Alaska and give talks, telling the folks out in the bush about what's goin' on back here at the association. Ain't that just gonna be a kick? I guess they was just lookin' for someone that ain't afraid a talkin' to people." Elsie hugged herself, then threw a kiss toward Brenda.

"Yessir, I sure got what I was wantin' outa this here class, plus I got all you for friends and that sweet little gal for a almost daughter." Elsie giggled and wiped a tear from her eye when everyone stood and applauded her final speech.

Martha's Farewell

Jo Massey

From the window in my shop attached to the end of my garage I can see the black asphalt ribbon coming south from Tulsa. When I heard a vehicle turn off the highway and onto the county road, I glanced up from a pile of shiny rocks I'd emptied from the rock tumbler moments earlier.

A silver Mercedes moved slowly along the road, stopped, then pulled in at my gate and crept to a stop in front of the house. I knew by the car, not the driving, that it was Toots. Normally, when she visits, it takes the dust a full five minutes to settle after she's sped up the lane, pulled to a screeching halt throwing cinders in every direction, and she's jumped out and flung her arms around my neck. But today she sat leaning dispiritedly across the steering wheel before emerging.

I watched her long legs unfold and, as always, wondered how a skirt could be so short yet still manage to cover her tush. I thought it was a bit disgraceful for a woman—of what? had to be forty-something—to dress like that, even though, lord knows, she still had the legs for it. But then, what do I know? I'm just an old bachelor.

"Uncle Irving, I've missed you," she said, giving me a peck on the cheek, her heady perfume sending my sinuses into convulsions.

"Hello, Toots," I said. "Have a seat." I indicated the stool where I'd been sitting examining the stones.

"Thanks." She plopped down on it, and I expected her to cross her legs, revealing, as was her custom, even more thigh. But she didn't. Instead she planted both feet on the bottom rung and leaned her elbows on the workbench.

The Cordova girls have always called me "uncle," even though we're not blood kin. Henry, their father, and I were best friends all our growing up years. He married Cora, his high school sweetheart, and they had the three girls—Regina, Katherine, and Eileen. I expect I'm the only one who still remembers that Toots' real name is Eileen—don't think anyone's ever been allowed to call her that.

When the Korean War came along, Henry signed up. Cora and I begged him not to, but he had a stubborn streak—not to mention extreme patriotism passed down from his father—and besides, he reasoned, his family could use the extra money. He couldn't be dissuaded.

I'll never forget the last words he ever spoke to me. "Funny thing," he'd said. "I've always thought how unlucky it was for you—polio leaving you crippled like it did. But that just might be the luck that saves your life—keeping you out of this war. Funny, huh?"

That day I didn't think it was funny. I was angry with him—married with kids—going off to fight a war in a foreign land, looking handsome in his new uniform, and me, with no family, sitting at home doing nothing.

After word came from the Army about their daddy, I tried to help with the raising of his girls. I could've done a better job of it if Cora hadn't dragged them off up to Tulsa a few years later. I guess that's a lame excuse for the guilt I carry about the way they turned out, not that they're really all that bad now that they're grown.

I looked at the woman sitting on my stool idly fingering a smooth stone from the pile, an inscrutable expression on her flawlessly painted face.

"Something troubling you?" I asked, knowing full well something was.

"Oh, Uncle Irving," she sighed. "I feel so ashamed."

Well, this should really be good, I thought. I know lots of things that she's done in her life that she should be ashamed about, but apparently isn't. What, I wondered, had finally brought her to such an admission. I waited, but knowing her so well, I could see she wanted to be coaxed.

"Want to tell me about it?" I clumsily patted her shoulder, a gesture that felt strange to me, but she seemed to need reassurance.

She turned to look at me, the hint of a smile softening the harsh lines around her eyes for a moment. "You don't think I drove all the way down here to not tell you, do you?" she teased.

If she'd been a religious woman, I suspect she'd have long since thrown me over for a good priest as her confidante, confessor, and counselor, but she hadn't. Playing those roles to her has had its drawbacks, to be sure, but they've also provided me with hours of amusing, real-life anecdotes.

"Do you have anything a thirsty girl could drink?"

"Iced tea."

She made a wry face. "Is that all?"

When I nodded, she said, "Well, then, how about bringing me a little glass of ice. I have something in the car."

When I got back to the shop, she was again perched on the stool, looking at one of the polished stones through a bottle of bourbon. "Look," she said, laughing, "This plain white quartz looks almost like gold when you view it through booze."

I couldn't see it, but didn't say so.

"It's a little like what happened," she said, uncapping the bottle and pouring a generous amount of amber liquid over the ice.

She was about to begin her story, so I pulled a crate up close, sat down, and took a sip of my tea.

"Aunt Martha died, you know."

A sudden jolt that hit me in the pit of my stomach, and the sharpness of it rather surprised me, but I held a straight face. No, I didn't know. Nobody had informed me. Martha, Henry's sister, had been gone from Oklahoma more years than I wanted to think about.

"Really?" I said. "Was she still living in Alaska?"

"Yes. Retired a couple of years back, an old maid schoolteacher. Never married, don't ask me why. She always said it was because she was so fat and homely, but I never believed that, did you?"

I shrugged. True, she'd not been as good-looking as most of the other members of Henry's family. But she'd made up for it with many other redeemable qualities.

"She got cancer. One of her friends called to tell us she died, so—us being her only family—we wanted to do the proper thing. The girls and I grabbed a plane and flew up there to go to her funeral. We just got back a few days ago."

"I'm sorry to hear it," I said. "That she died, I mean." I knew by 'the girls' she meant her sisters.

"Yes, well, it was quite the experience," she sighed, and for several moments continued staring at the piece of quartz through the bottle.

Ice tinkled in her glass as she lifted it to her lips and took a drink. Her fingernails, very long, blunt on the ends, painted a deep burgundy, had little gold stars imbedded in some of them. Fascinating, I thought. They looked awkward to me. I wondered how she managed with them, doing other people's hair and nails every day, dialing the phone, even opening her own car door. But what would an old bachelor know about such things?

Normally, once she starts a story, it's like pulling a snag on a sweater—it just unravels in one long, continuous string. Now, she sat there nervously tapping her nails against her glass. I waited, but this time it seemed she needed more encouragement from me before she'd continue.

Finally I said, "I'm waiting."

She looked at me slowly, as if trying to refocus her eyes from her reverie to the present moment.

"Well, Katz and I flew together to Seattle where we had a long layover before catching the red-eye special on into Anchorage. We wanted to be early enough to meet Reggie's plane when it came in from Detroit. We hadn't seen her in four or five years—not since she married that farmer fellow. We almost didn't recognize her—she's let herself go so bad. Stopped coloring her hair, put on extra pounds, and she was wearing just a plain old ordinary cotton dress and flat-heeled shoes. It was a shock, I tell you."

I did have a hard time imagining the oldest and most infamous of the "siren sisters" becoming dowdy. Why, by thirteen she had a reputation that was—well, let's just say I was glad when Cora left that year and took the embarrassing girl with her.

"So Katz and I gathered her up, caught us a cab straight to the nearest shopping mall, found a salon, and, after giving the operator a sob story about having to catch a plane right away to go to poor Aunt Martha's funeral, we got Reggie right into a chair. Red, we told the beautician. Make her hair red. She did and it turned out beautiful, really very beautiful. Next we made her buy some decent clothes. Foundation garments, first. Do you know what I mean, Uncle Irving, by foundation garments?"

I nodded, feeling a bit irked. I may be just an old bachelor, but I'm not totally naïve. I have seen a mail order catalog or two in my day, and I know what women's underwear is called.

"Well, what she needed was not just your plain ordinary underwear. She had a few blobs and rolls that had to be sucked in and tightened up before she was even presentable! We didn't let up on her until we finally found one of those one-piece girdle contraptions that cover everything from boobs to butt. I was disgusted with her and told her so. One thing we Cordovas have always prided ourselves in is our tight little buns. Mine are still as firm as the day I turned fifteen, don't you think?"

She hopped off the stool and turned her back to me, swaying her hips from side to side. I couldn't help thinking they resembled two marshmallows on top of willow twigs, ready for roasting. I'd always preferred more fleshy female posteriors. When she peered over her shoulder at me with teasing hazel eyes, I looked away, embarrassed, and swirled the ice in my tea.

She laughed, kissed me lightly on the forehead, and slid back onto the stool. "Anyway, later I was sorry I'd made such a big issue of it because it made Reggie feel bad. She even cried, had mascara running down her cheeks and everything, if you can imagine. But, then we bought her a couple of outfits that were quite flattering, especially with her red hair, and she perked up.

"We still had an hour or so to kill before the plane left, so we stopped in an airport bar. There was a group of Seattle bank executives waiting for our same flight and they bought us several drinks. They said they were going to Anchorage on business, but, as we suspected and later discovered to be true, all their business was monkey business. All of them, especially one, were hot on Katz right away. She is so stunning in her platinum blond hair and expensive clothes."

I was sure that the last time I'd seen Katherine her hair was jet black. Stunning? Shocking, actually, would be the word I'd more than likely use to describe the haughtiest of the three.

"Once they discovered she was a massage therapist, they really swarmed around her. Seems they all had big plans to visit as many massage parlors in Anchorage as possible. When Katz insisted that hers was a legitimate business, they laughed and said so were the ones in Anchorage. Then they winked at each other. One tried to pinch her and she slapped his hand, playfully, and put on that pouty look, until they agreed that hers was on the up and up. And, before long, she had them totally mesmerized again with her wit and charm. She's so aggravating, really. I should hate her. Here she is a full four years older than me, but she looks at least ten years younger. She's had a face-lift, a boob lift, butt lift, a tummy tuck. Why, she's had so many 'lifts' that if she has even one more, I swear, her feet won't touch the ground."

I laughed. "Must have gotten at least one lift, so-to-speak, out of every husband." I'd lost track of the number of marriages she'd had.

"Yeah, that and half his bank account," Toots said. "The girl is loaded. Rich, beautiful, sexy. I should hate her, really."

"Well," I said, pointing at her Mercedes, "it doesn't look like you are doing so poorly yourself."

"Oh, I know. But I've had to earn everything myself. All the guys I get involved up with seem to be losers." She drained her glass and refilled it from the bottle.

I'd been privileged to meet some of them and had to agree. "Need more ice?" I asked.

She shook her head. "So, anyway, we were all feeling relaxed by the time we loaded onto the plane. As it turned out our seats were right in amongst the bankers and they kept buying us drinks the whole distance."

"It was just after midnight in Anchorage—let's see,

I think that would have made it about four in the morning here—and we were so wiped out we'd forgotten where we were or even why we were there, until some big somber-faced man in a black suit came up and asked us if we were the relatives of Miss Martha Jean Cordova." Her use of Martha's full name brought a dull thud in my heart and a flood of memories, but I tried to push them away. This wasn't the time to indulge in thoughts of my own. My thoughts and feelings, where Martha is concerned, I've always kept to myself alone.

"Seems he'd been sent by her friends to help us make connections to her village on a tiny little bush plane scheduled to leave at seven in the morning. That was Tuesday. We hadn't made reservations to stay over anywhere, so our new acquaintances invited us to wile away those few hours with them. Which we gladly did." She winked and grinned mischievously.

Such goings on are still shocking to me, even though I know it's tolerated these days. I wondered, but only briefly, if this was what she was so ashamed of.

"Don't give me that squinched up face, Uncle Irving. We're adults. Besides nothing happened, at least not that any of us remembered, including the men. And, believe me, if they'd tangled with any one of us they would not have forgotten."

Her laugh told more than I cared to know. I stood and started toward the house, more acutely aware of my limp than normal for some reason, perhaps remembering how Martha had always seemed to be able to ignore it.

"Where you going?" she asked.

"To take a leak and get more tea. Do you want me to bring you something?"

"More ice would be nice. Do you have anything to snack on? Chips or crackers, maybe?"

When I got back to the shop she was stubbing a cigarette out on the concrete floor. "I see you've started smoking again," I said.

"Only sometimes. Like now, when I'm nervous or upset."

She put on such a good front a person had to really know her to detect when she was upset or nervous. I did, of course, so I changed the subject by offering her the plate with crackers and cheese. "Here's a snack," I said and helped myself to a couple of crackers. "So, did you get back to the airport in time to catch the bush plane?"

She picked up a square of cheese and mashed it around in her mouth before saying, "Oh yeah. But I certainly wished afterwards that we hadn't. Reggie got sick all over the inside of it. You've got to understand that the plane was so tiny it only held the pilot and the three of us. Katz even had to leave two of her bags in a locker at the airport. Of course, she always takes enough stuff on a trip to stay for months, so leaving some of it behind wasn't a big deal. She thought it was, though, and whined about it the whole time. Between her whining, Reggie vomiting, that toy plane bouncing all over the sky, the pilot screaming for us all to shut-up and my throbbing headache, it was the worst two hours I believe I've ever spent in my entire life."

Wow, I thought, remembering all the other 'worst' times I'd heard about. I felt a twinge of pity for the poor pilot and wondered if he'd made a mental note to be off-duty the day they returned.

"Everybody in the whole village was there to watch the plane land. Come to see the three nieces of their beloved teacher, and all of us just looking and feeling like shit! It was Katz, as usual, who took in the whole scope of things, and stepped from the plane looking like some foreign princess—her platinum head held high and regal—waving to the crowd in that windshield-wiper motion, just like she was some celebrity. All the while under her breath, behind her smiling lips and clenched teeth, she's bitching at us to fix ourselves up and get on out there."

I smiled, knowing that Toots always thought she looked like 'shit' anytime she didn't believe she looked like a perfectly painted porcelain doll.

"Were the natives friendly?" I couldn't resist asking.

"They were bereft. Truly bereft," she said, as if surprised. "It would have touched your heart, Uncle Irving. It was surprising to see how much they loved that old woman." I'd known Martha well, and, no, it didn't surprise me at all.

One of Toots' star-studded fingers toyed with a piece of ice in her drink, guiding it around the edge of the glass. She sucked the moisture off her finger before taking a drink. "The local postmaster, a Mister Willmer, also served as the mortician. A colorless man—was at first, anyway, until we got to know him better—is also the only white man living in the village. We were terribly disappointed, at first. You always hear about how many more men there are than women in Alaska, and we expected white men, of course. There were plenty of wizened-up, old snaggle-toothed, pruned-faced, bowlegged natives. I guess maybe that's what made Willmer finally take on a better glow in our minds. Before the whole shindig was over, there was Reggie shagging up to him, and—what's worse—neither me nor Katz thinking a thing of it. But I'm getting ahead of myself."

She looked at me as if expecting some negative response. She didn't know that I couldn't have cared less what Regina or Katherine did. I was patiently waiting for her to get to her shameful part.

"It was about noon by the time all the greetings were done and our bags had been taken to the dumpy clapboard rooming house where we were to stay. Willmer wanted to take us straight away to see Aunt Martha laid out—of all places—in the cooler at the one little grocery store. He'd even set up a formal 'viewing' for the whole village, between one and four o'clock. Can you even imagine? We begged him to please let us get some rest before we had to go through that ordeal. So, 'in deference to the three lovely visitors from the lower 48,' as he put it, the viewing was postponed until five o'clock."

She took a cracker and then was quiet for some time. I sensed the story was finally getting somewhere near the climax and her point of confession. I leisurely sipped my tea, waiting. She again seemed to want some show of encouragement on my part, but I decided to let her sweat a little. If it was worth driving all the way down here to be absolved, then it deserved some discomfort.

When she spoke, her voice was little and pinched, reminding me of the time, when she was only three or four, she'd brought me her kitten, found smashed on the highway, thinking somehow that I could make it well. That voice betrayed the depth of her feelings.

"Thankfully, Willmer let the girls and me in before the others. It was awful, Uncle Irving, just the god-awfulest thing I've ever seen in my whole life. There in the casket, instead of that jolly-fat woman I remembered, was this shrunk-up, gray-haired, sallow-faced, ugly little thing. Still homely, but no longer fat. And not a hint of makeup anywhere on her. I've been to funerals where I thought whoever had done the makeup had done such a horrid job they needed training at a good beauty school. But I've never seen a dead body without any makeup."

She gulped from her glass and plunged ahead with the story. A lump was forming in my throat, and I was beginning to be sorry I'd encouraged her to tell the story in such vivid detail.

"We were in total shock until Willmer said something about letting the rest of them in to look. In the same instant, we all three screeched 'NO!' He looked at us like we were crazy. 'Why?' he wanted to know. We stared at him, not able to believe he didn't realize he'd forgotten to get someone to fix her up. When we told him that, he stared back at us like he'd never heard of such a cockamamie idea.

"Katz, bless her heart, tried in her most diplomatic way to explain it to him in terms he would understand. 'When people want to send a letter to someone special and want it to get to them quickly, what do they do?' she asked him. When he shrugged, she said—in that voice she uses when she tries to say something so simple a little child would understand, 'Well, they put it in a pretty colored envelope, maybe draw little pictures around the edges, and put an airmail stamp on it!' I guess it's been awhile since she mailed anything," Toots added.

"Willis gave her a blank look and said, 'Well, all the folks here use plain white envelopes and everything automatically goes airmail from here since there aren't any roads. Besides, what does that have to do with Martha?'"

I had to agree with this Willmer guy. I couldn't see the connection either.

"We could see we weren't getting anywhere with this," Toots continued, "so, we asked him where we could find a beautician. He laughed then. Laughed until I thought he'd pass out. 'There's one about seven hundred miles to the east of here, in Fairbanks,' he said, pointing with one hand and holding his gut with the other. Then he went outside and told the people standing around that the viewing was off, they'd just all have to wait until the funeral tomorrow."

I realized she had me in the spell of her story when I took a drink of tea and choked. I hadn't been aware that she'd poured bourbon into my glass as well as her own. We both took another sip. I grimaced and for a moment tried to remember just how long it'd been since I gave up drinking.

"They held a wake for her later that night, and we were expected to be there, of course. We got all dolled up for it, wanting to be proper representation of her family. Reggie looked fabulous in her new jade-green dress, her red hair piled in curls on top of her head. I wore that little pink suit with the short skirt and beaded jacket. It always gets admiring looks—shows off my tan nicely. But I'll have to admit, even with my tan I felt pale in that crowd of brown-skinned natives. Katz, as always, outdid us both in her virgin white pantsuit, trimmed with gold buttons and bangles."

She slid from the stool and excused herself to go 'to the powder room'. I limped into the kitchen, poured out the vile drink, refilled my glass with tea, and waited for her to come out of the bathroom. "Do you want to sit in here now?" I asked when she finally emerged.

"Sure." She slumped into my leather recliner, tucking one leg under herself. "Where did I leave off?"

I pulled out the straight back chair by my writing desk and sat down. "You were going to a wake, I think," I said.

"Oh, yes, that's right. This was my first wake, you know. Biggest damn party I think I've ever been to," she said.

Hmm, I doubted that but kept my thoughts to myself.

"At first we felt kind of out of place, the only white women there, dressed like we were going to church or something, with everyone else wearing jeans and sweatshirts. Those folks sure know how to drink, I tell you. Dance, too. They do an Eskimo shuffle thing that's just a bunch of stomping around in a circle. It looked silly at first, especially with us in our stupid high heels and them wearing leather moccasins, or whatever they call them." She laughed, remembering. "But it got to be kind of fun once we'd kicked off our shoes and had a couple of more drinks."

She looked to see if I was disapproving, but I smiled back encouragingly. There was a long pause as she examined her nails.

"We'd had too much to drink," she admitted, letting the words hang in the air. A look I couldn't quite read crossed her face—sort of a combination of shame and sadness. "That's where the real problem started."

Good, I thought. Finally, we're getting down to the confession part. I waited, giving her time.

"At first these people couldn't understand why we'd had the 'viewing' called off. They couldn't see any reason a dead person needed to be fixed up, just to be buried. But when we explained that in our culture that's what we do, they were all for it. In fact, it was one of them who suggested we do it ourselves. They even wanted to help."

I could sense where the story was going, and I already began to feel repulsed.

"The more we talked about it, the more we drank. The more we drank, the better the idea sounded. Even Willmer got behind it, probably more to try to impress Reggie than for any other reason. Anyway, about midnight the whole party traipses out first to the boarding house to get our makeup bags, then on over to the store. The owner, of course, is with us, as is everyone in the whole village except maybe some kids. He opens it up; we all go into the cooler where poor Aunt Martha is chilling and proceed to get her ready."

I began wishing I hadn't poured out my spiked tea, thinking I might need a stiffer drink myself to bear hearing the rest of this story.

"I felt a little squeamish at first so I tried to get one of the other girls to do the job. But, no. 'You're the beautician,' they insisted, 'the expert,' so it was only natural that I be the one to do it. Then everyone started partying again, laughing and singing and talking and drinking. It actually did turn into fun. When I was done, they all said how beautiful she looked. Then everyone walked us back to the hotel, now all friends, and we said good night. Reggie went on home with Willmer, but that's another story."

She suddenly jumped up, went out and returned with her bottle. As she poured bourbon over fresh ice, I waited and wondered what the rest of the tale would reveal. I can't say how sorry I was feeling for dear Martha.

"The funeral was supposed to start at two o'clock the next day. We found out too late that nothing ever starts on time, so there we were for nearly an hour, still a little hung-over but decent, sitting in the front row of the tiny Russian Orthodox Church, the only church in town. By the time the service started, it was packed. I guess everyone in the borough was there. That's what they call their counties in Alaska. Did you know that?"

I nodded. I did know that from Martha's letters.

"The priest had to come in from a mission somewhere else to perform the service. It was all very formal and quite lovely. Anyway, what we could remember of it was lovely, we decided later."

"That's nice," I said, feeling some relief. "I'm glad she had a nice Christian service. She really was a good woman."

Toots gave me a rather wry look, then she continued, her voice now barely audible. "When the service was finished, the last song sung, the last prayer prayed, they opened the casket and folks started filing by it on their way out of the church. It seemed to us like people were acting a little strange, almost like they were choking or something—but we'd already seen that they do lots of strange things. So we didn't really think much of it. That is, not until it was our turn. As her family, you know, we were the last to leave."

I held my breath, not wanting to know, yet something kept me from stopping her. I felt sick as I listened to the pitiful end of her tale.

"Oh, Uncle Irving, she looked like bozo the clown on a bad day! It was so horrible. White face powder was caked all over her face, even in her hair. Lipstick was smeared clear up under her nose, round red globs of rouge spread practically all the way from her nose to her ears. Her penciled-in eyebrows were like two black teepees, halfway up her forehead. I'd even put a brown 'beauty mark' on her chin, so big it looked like a wad of chew. Oh, she looked absolutely hideous. Katz and Reggie placed all the blame on me, of course, saying how I was the expert and all that. They screamed about it all the way back to Seattle—even threatened to call all my customers and tell them. They were serious, too! And now they won't even speak to me."

I started to say something soothing, but before I could think what that could possibly be, she plunged on, talking faster. Without taking a breath, her words tumbled out in such a jumble I had a hard time following along.

"I was so embarrassed I started bawling on the spot because I've worked so hard to build up a good reputation—you know, a good clientele—I can just imagine what my clients will do if Katz and Reggie tell them because I know they'll drop me like a shitty diaper and go somewhere else and then I'll just be completely destroyed and have to move away somewhere and start over again because my reputation has taken years to build and it is more important to me than anything else I can think of." She ran out of breath, gulped in another and continued, "Oh, God, I'm so ashamed. Here I am, the professional, doing such a despicable job, taking a chance on ruining myself and all for just a stinking old corpse! "

I was incredulous. She wasn't ashamed of making a mockery of Martha. This was all about her. I suddenly began to shake, anger taking control. "Get out," I said, trying to hold my voice steady.

"What?" she asked. "Uncle Irving, what do you mean?"

"Leave, Eileen," I said, deliberately using her given name, knowing it would infuriate her. I didn't care. I turned away, not trusting my emotions. For long moments there was dead silence. Then I heard the leather of the chair crinkle as she left it. Her steps crossed the linoleum kitchen floor, the back door opened and slammed shut. I walked to the window and watched her jam the car in reverse, back up and spin around to head down the driveway, just barely missing the wall of my shop. Her face looked pale when she glanced toward the house before peeling down the lane, throwing cinders in every direction.

When I was sure she was gone, I opened the lower drawer of my writing desk and pulled out the photo. The plain cardboard frame has frayed and faded over the years. But the eyes of the girl are still as blue as the simple taffeta gown she's wearing. The youthful couple stands inside a big heart-shaped frame. Class of 1939 is painted onto the frame in purple and white, our school colors. Anymore, I scarcely resemble the young man with my arm around her.

I sat in my recliner a long time, watching shadows move across the walls as the day faded from afternoon to dusk, cradling the photo in my hands. When I rose and turned on the lamp, all traces of the afternoon's tears were only dried smears on the frame.

White-Out

Everything was white—the road, the air, the car, her face, her knuckles. The Alaska Highway we traveled was snow-packed, probably had been for months now. The road was long and boring, broken only by frequent, deep drifts of snow, and once in a while a scrubby fir that reminded me of Charlie Brown's pitiful Christmas tree. The air surrounding us was white—either bursts of new-falling snow or great puffy clouds of powder swirling up as we passed. This is what's called a "white out," where you can't tell one thing from another because they all look the same. It's almost blinding. Our car, the big Chrysler Dad was so proud of, was entirely white also, all except the dark green leather seats, which added the only bit of color.

But Mom was whitest of all. Her face was drawn and tense, her lips pressed tight into a straight line. Her dark eyes stared straight ahead, and once, when she hadn't blinked for what seemed like a full minute, I thought she might be in a trance. She was gripping the steering wheel so tightly I wondered if she would ever be able to open her hands all the way again. I'd never seen anyone's knuckles look like hers did; it startled me to see the round white patches, looking almost like bare bone, pushing out of the pinkish flesh of her hands. She was worried. It was plain to see.

I looked away from her face for a minute and glanced into the back seat where my three sisters sat. Terrie, eleven and three years younger than me, stared out the side window, although I knew there was nothing for her to see. She hated to travel and only tolerated the long drive because it was the only way she could get back home to her world of friends. Darlene, eight going on eighteen, was patiently reading a book. She turned a page as I watched, obviously very absorbed and apparently unaware of the horrible road and weather. Jodie, a lively five-year-old and the baby of the family, was between my sisters, curled into a ball in the center seat, sleeping.

I wished I could sleep or even relax, but as the eldest daughter, I felt a responsibility to help keep Mom awake. If she dozed off, I was ready to grab the steering wheel so I could bring us to a safe stop. I didn't have a driver's license, of course—that had to wait a couple of more years—but Dad had occasionally let me practice on back roads, so I knew the basics of steering and braking. Thinking of Dad made me homesick, and I, too, wished we were safely home. Unfortunately, we still had a long ways to go—we were only about two-thirds of the way between Everett, Washington, where we'd spent the holidays with our grandparents, and home—a five-day trip in good weather. With this weather, we could plan on six or more.

The trip going "outside" had gone smoothly, with good weather all the way. Dad was with us then, too, which made it seem easier. But he'd had a call about an emergency situation from his job at home and flew back the day after Christmas. Mom assured him that we "girls" would be fine, that she was a good driver and had lots of experience. He agreed this was true, but warned her to be extra careful on the drive home.

We'd stopped night before last in Whitehorse, Yukon Territory. Somehow it always seemed like we'd nearly made it home once we reached that outpost, but I knew it was still two or three more days of driving.

That next morning, the car hadn't started, even though the head bolt engine heater had been plugged in all night. We'd had to have a tow truck come to thaw out the engine. The man jacked up the front end, threw a tarp over it, and then heated it from underneath with a big Herman Nelson space heater. When we left Whitehorse, the temperature was sixty below zero, and when we stopped for lunch at a lodge along the way, their thermometer said it was a minus seventy-five.

When we stopped last night at another lodge after driving all day, I was worried about the car starting again. But a man who worked there told us that a storm was coming in. The temperatures were expected to warm up and with it would come clouds and snow.

Sure enough, by this morning the temperature had risen and it was around twenty below zero. That was a relief.

Mom went out to warm up the car while we ate breakfast. It didn't want to start at first, in spite of being plugged in all night. But when she took the lid off the carburetor and sprayed a little ether in it, it started right up. She always carries a can of ether just for that reason.

"What if the car stops while we're driving?" I asked nervously.

"We just have to keep it running," Mom said. "We won't shut it off for anything." On this entire trip she'd left it running any time we stopped to go into a lodge to eat or use the bathroom, only shutting it off long enough to fill with gas.

By the time we'd finished breakfast and were ready to leave, it was spitting snow. Several hours later, the snow had begun to come down hard. The wipers flapped rapidly back and forth in a steady rhythm across the windshield, but it barely kept the window clear enough to see. My side fogged over until I had only a peephole in the center, about as big as my fist, even though the heater fan was going full blast. I felt sleepy, almost hypnotized by the motion of the blades.

I forcefully jerked myself awake, and looked again at Mom. She was leaning forward, trying to see through a small hole cleared in her windshield. Her lips, even tighter than before, looked like an invisible zipper sealing shut her lower face. It felt like we were merely crawling.

I was so intrigued by her look of total concentration that I didn't see what was happening. Suddenly a flash of shock crossed her face. Instantly she jammed on the brake and swerved toward the right. Then, just as fast, she twisted the steering wheel sharply to the left, but the car seemed to have a mind of its own, because it didn't obey. Instead of turning left, it kept going right; snow flew past the windows as we jolted to a sudden stop.

She quickly slid the gearshift into reverse, pushed on the gas—hard—but nothing happened. The engine sputtered and died. Everything went quiet. A look of panic was in her eyes when she met my gaze.

"Why'd we stop here?" Terrie asked, sitting up with interest, her bored expression suddenly gone.

Darlene laid her book aside, and tried to see out the window. "Can we get out and stretch?"

"I'm hungry," Jodie said, sitting up and rubbing sleep from her eyes. "Are we at a restaurant?"

"There's no restaurant here. There's nothing here," Terrie said, sounding irritated and confused.

We all stared at Mom, but she ignored our questions as she tried to start the car.

"Is the car broke?" Jodie asked. She was quite awake now.

"What happened? Why did you drive off the road?" Darlene—always the practical one—asked. She'll be a lawyer someday is what we always say. She has all the questions and won't give up until she's gotten answers to all of them.

Mom kept cranking the starter, trying to coax the engine back to life.

"Be quiet, all of you," I said, "so Mom can concentrate."

"There was a moose in the road," she finally answered. "Suddenly he was just there, standing in the middle of the road, looming up out of the snowstorm. I had to swerve to miss him, and when I did, the front wheels hit the snow berm at the edge of the road and it sucked us into the ditch. I'm afraid we're really stuck."

"What are we going to do?" I asked. I tried to sound businesslike, afraid of upsetting my sisters if I let them know how really scared I was.

"Maybe, if I can get the car started again, we can rock it back and forth and get out of the ditch," Mom said. She sounded mechanical, like she wasn't a real person, more like a robot. The look on her face scared me even more than I already was.

"What if it won't start?" Terrie's voice quivered. Instead of looking bored or cranky, she now seemed about to cry.

"Maybe the car just needs to rest a minute," Mom said. "I'll get out and see if I can figure out what's wrong."

She looked at me hard for a long moment. I knew she was really worried, but after a minute I saw her slide on her "got it all under control mask" as Dad calls it. I'm usually comforted when I see her in that face, but this time I wasn't. I knew we were in deep trouble.

Her voice was calm when she asked me, "Where are we? Do you remember what milepost we last passed?"

I was her co-pilot; my job was to follow the "milepost" guidebook and keep track of where the next gas and food would be available.

I'd been so anxious about the road conditions that I'd forgotten to watch the markers for the last hour or so. I felt my face flush, embarrassed that I couldn't think. Then I did remember that we'd passed a lodge a few miles back. The driveway was piled high with snow and a sign across the gate had said, "Closed for the winter." I'd thought it was a little strange that it was closed since I could see smoke coming from the chimney and snowmobile tracks all over the place.

I opened the book and turned to a page where I'd left the bookmark my boyfriend had given me for Christmas. He'd hand tooled the leather himself, and it usually made me happy to see it, but this time I didn't even notice it. It marked the place we'd last gotten gas, maybe five hours ago. I wracked my brain to recall exactly how far back that had been. Mom was watching me patiently.

"I don't know how far back it was, but I think the closed lodge was this one," I said, pointing in the book, "but I'm not sure." I felt rattled, realizing how important this was and feeling bad that I'd not been paying better attention.

"Okay," she said. "Let's try figuring it another way. Where did we last buy gas?"

I showed her where I'd left the bookmark.

She looked at the gas gauge. "We have about a quarter of a tank left. We usually get about 360 miles to a tank, which would mean we've maybe come 270 miles since we filled up." She took the book from me and studied the pages. At last she handed it back.

"If my guess is correct, we are still about a hundred miles from Tok Junction, at the Alaska/Canada border. If that is true, the next lodge is somewhere between thirty and forty miles ahead, and the closed one we passed was probably ten miles back. Too far to walk for help."

I gulped and nodded. "That seems about how far it was. I'm really sorry I wasn't keeping better track, Mom." I couldn't stop the tear from springing free.

She reached across the seat and patted my hand. "It's all right, Lynne," she said. "Now we just have to figure out how to get ourselves out of this mess."

She turned to look at the little girls in the back seat, who were being very quiet, sober expressions on all their faces. "We're going to be okay," Mom said, trying to reassure them. "Put your coats on and button them up so you'll stay warm. I'm going outside to see if I can figure out how to get the car going again."

She lifted the handle for the door and gave a push, but it wouldn't open. She tried again, still without success. She turned the key on so the window would work, and lowered it a couple of inches. Snow was packed tight against it, and some broke off and fell in, landing on her shoulder and lap. She quickly rolled the window back up.

"Try your door, honey," she said softly, nodding to me. I pulled up on the handle and shoved hard. No matter how hard I pushed, my door wouldn't open either.

Her eyes were larger than usual when she looked at me. "I think we're buried." She whispered the words, obviously trying not to alarm the younger girls.

I wished she hadn't used that word. I remembered the safety film we'd been shown at school, where some cross-country skiers were buried alive in an avalanche. I tried hard not to imagine how that would feel. The thought made me feel creepy.

Darlene began to cry, huge tears coursing silently down her cheek. She'd heard Mom's words, because she'd leaned forward and was wedged up against the front seat.

"What's wrong?" Jodie asked her, alarmed and startled by her sister's silent sobs. "Why are you crying?" she insisted, then she noisily started her own frightened wailing.

Terrie didn't say a word, but she had a stricken look on her face when she met my eyes. Tears were brimming in her eyes also. "We're buried alive? We're going to die?" she asked hoarsely.

Her words chilled me, and I suddenly realized how serious this whole thing was. I could feel fear rising in my own body. A wave of panic washed over me and without intending to, tears scalded my cheeks. I felt very childish and ashamed.

When I looked back at Mom, she was staring out the windshield as if she could see an answer there. "No, we are not going to die," she said almost sternly. "We just have a challenge that needs to be met."

She was always so positive about everything, and I often wondered if she really believed everything was as cheery as she pretended it was. But this time I really hoped she was right. "I just need to have a minute to think," she said.

"I'll try my door," Darlene said brightly. She's going to be just like Mom when she grows up—nothing will bother her. She pulled on the latch and pushed. The door opened just a fraction, but would go no farther. Well, at least that was something.

Terrie followed Darlene's example, working with her door. Her looks of boredom had long since fled. She pushed on it and it opened all the way! We all cheered!

Icy vapor filled the car as the freezing air met our warm breath, and for a minute we couldn't see each other.

Terrie started to get out, but Mom stopped her. "No, you girls stay in the car where it's still warm. I'll crawl over the seat and get out to have a look." She took the keys from the ignition and clumsily scrambled over the seat.

The three girls squeezed together on Darlene's side of the car to make room for Mom to crawl out.

We couldn't see anything outside, but I heard her digging around in the trunk. In a few moments Mom opened the door and started shoving things in—sweaters, socks, extra pairs of jeans, blankets, sleeping bags, boxes of crackers and other snack foods—making several trips to the trunk. The temperature in the car dipped each time the door was opened.

"Put on the extra clothes," she said. "Then crawl into a sleeping bag or wrap up in one of the blankets. And snuggle close together." We did as she said, feeling like over-stuffed animals.

"How bad is it?" I asked when she'd finished bringing things from the trunk and had crawled back into the front seat.

"There is nothing we can do. We will just have to wait for help to come," she said. "When we hit that berm, it completely sucked the car into the deep snow in the ditch. Only the left rear is showing. The rest of the car is packed so tight, it'd take a giant can opener to get us out."

"How long do you think we'll have to wait for help," I asked. I tried to recall how long it had been since we'd even met another car on the road. We'd made a game of it earlier, counting how many cars we met. Yesterday there had been five, today only two so far.

"Only a fool would be on the road in temperatures and weather like this," the mechanic had said yesterday when he'd helped get the car running. Mom had agreed with him, but she said we had to get home in time for us girls to start school again on Monday.

"Someone will be by soon," she told us, but I knew there was no way for her to know that. It was her eternal optimism speaking, but I was glad, for the sake of my sisters, that she was giving us hope.

We sat miserably. Terrie was back in her bored mood, sighing audibly now and again, with her eyes closed.

Darlene had tried to read, but it was too cold to hold her book, and she seemed quiet and worried now, sitting with her eyes shut. Jodie whispered sleepily to her stuffed monkey snuggled in her arms. I closed my eyes and tried to think about anything else but our situation—my friends at school, what I got for Christmas, my grandparents, and, of course, my boyfriend.

I was beginning to drift off when suddenly Mom said, "We mustn't all fall asleep. Someone has to stay awake. It is very important."

I thought again about the safety film. I seemed to recall that it had warned against falling asleep when you were very cold. One of the warning signs of freezing to death was becoming sleepy and lethargic. Hypothermia they called it. My heart beat faster and I was suddenly wide-awake.

"Let's sing," I suggested. We had lots of songs we sang when we traveled to keep us from getting bored.

"Great idea," Mom said. The younger girls squirmed and sat up, even Terrie.

We sang *Row, Row, Row Your Boat*, and *Hey Ho*, and *Three Blind Mice*, and *The Farmer in the Dell*, and *Little Bunny Foo-Foo*, and *The Ants Go Marching*. Time passed and nobody came by.

We sang more. *On Top of Spaghetti* and *Hole in the Bottom of the Sea.* Mom even let us do the long version of *Ninety-nine Bottles of Beer on the Wall.*

"I'm hungry," Jodie complained after a while.

"Me too," Terrie said.

"Okay, let's eat something," Mom said, and she began searching the bags of food she'd brought from the trunk. She handed out crackers and cheese, a little box of raisins each.

"Is there anything to drink?" I asked.

She shook her head. "Everything in the trunk was frozen solid, but we have some coffee in the thermos," she said, offering it to me.

"No thanks," I said. She offered it to the younger girls, but they all said no.

After we ate, we sang more songs. We did all the Christmas carols we'd recently been singing. When we were in the middle of *Joy to the World*, Mom suddenly stopped us by raising her hand. "Listen," she said.

We got quiet, and then I was sure I felt, maybe more than heard, an engine. The sound got closer, and it sounded like a truck. When it seemed to be right behind us, we all started shouting. But then the sound moved on and faded away down the road.

"Why didn't they stop?" we all seemed to ask in unison.

Mom looked stunned. "I was afraid of that," she said. "We are so deeply buried in the ditch that only the one door and a piece of the trunk are in view. It was still snowing when I was outside, too, so maybe the snow has covered up the rest of the car making it invisible. I knew we should have bought that other car—the blue one. Then maybe..." she trailed off.

"So, now what?" Terrie asked. Her voice sounded small and very scared.

"I'll get out again and see if I can make a flag out of something that will show up better," she said. She crawled over the seat again, and this time when she opened the door, it didn't seem any colder outside than it did inside.

When she got back in the car, she said the snow had finally stopped, but, as she guessed, the rest of the car had enough covering it to make it impossible to see. The vehicle that had gone past was a snowplow. It had scooped just one wide path out of the middle of the road. Maybe it would come back the other way soon. "I tied a pair of Dad's red longjohns to the antenna," she said. "That should make it easier for someone to see us."

The little bit of daylight inside of the car turned gloomy, and I knew it would be dark soon. I didn't want to spend the long night like this. None of us did, I knew that, but I was beginning to feel it was hopeless. Even our cheerful mom was quiet now.

After it got dark, we sang more songs, repeating some that we'd already sung. Then Mom started singing *Kumbah-yah.* She sang in her normal tone at first, and we followed along. Then her voice became softer, singing the words with more meaning. *"Someone's crying, Lord. Kumbah-yah. Someone's crying, Lord, Kumbah-yah..."* Then the next verse, *"Someone's praying, Lord, Kumbah-yah, someone's praying, Lord, Kumbah-yah..."*

I tried to see my sisters and Mom in the dark, but even though I couldn't, I sensed we were each touched by the song.

As the last chorus trailed away and we sat in the stillness of the moment, Mom said, "Maybe we should pray."

She'd sometimes taken us all to Sunday school when we were little, and I knew she was raised in church. But somehow, along the line, we'd stopped going. Dad said he believed that you could worship God just as well out in nature. So I was a little surprised by her suggestion.

"I don't remember how," Darlene said. I thought it was surprising for her to admit that she didn't know something. Then she corrected herself, "Well, I do know how, but I've forgotten the words."

"I remember how," Terrie said, her voice deep with conviction. She still went to church sometimes with her friends. "You just ask God for what you need."

"Yes, Terrie," Mom said. "That is what you do. You talk to Him like you would anybody else, telling Him what you need. Then you have to thank Him. The harder part is to have faith that He will answer your prayers."

"I can do it," Jodie suddenly piped up. In the dark I couldn't see her, but I knew she would be hugging her stuffed monkey; she's never without it.

"Okay," Mom said. "We can all take turns."

We waited for Jodie to begin, and then she finally said, "I don't know how to start."

"'Dear Jesus' is how you start," Terrie said.

"Dear Jesus, I'm cold and I'm hungry and I'm tired, but Lynne says I can't go to sleep or I will die," she prayed.

"Please make somebody come find us real soon." There was another silence. "How do I end it?"

"Say 'amen'," Terrie prompted.

"Amen," she said. "Oh, and thank you very much."

We each took turns, from the youngest up to the oldest. When it was my turn, I felt embarrassed at first, doing it in front of everyone else, but after the first few words I wasn't embarrassed anymore, and I prayed harder than I thought I could.

"Dear Jesus. I guess you know where we are, and how much we need to be rescued. It wasn't Mom's fault that we ran off the road. It was because of that moose, and she didn't want to hit it. Because of what she did that big ugly animal is still alive." I thought I heard someone giggle, but I ignored it and kept on. "It doesn't know the problem it caused and that we might die because of it. It's very cold, and the car won't run to keep us warm.

We don't have much food or anything to drink. It is very serious, and we need help, bad. Please send someone to save us."

I paused a long moment, trying to form the words I did, and yet didn't, want to say out loud. "Thank you for my Mom and my sisters. I love them all so much. And, if we have to die tonight, please let Dad and all our family and friends know that we love them, too. Amen."

When I finished, I knew Mom was crying; I could tell from her shoulders shaking. Whether it was from our prayers or whether she was that afraid, I don't know, but after a minute she prayed, too. Her prayer was longer than ours, more mature, like someone who still knew how to pray. She almost demanded that God send us help.

And she said, "Thank you, thank you, thank you," over and over again before saying "Amen."

We were all very quiet for several minutes after our prayers were finished.

Finally, Mom suggested I get in the back seat and switch places with Jodie. That way, because I am bigger, I could help keep the other two girls warmer, and Mom could cuddle with Jodie, Darlene, Terrie, and I huddled together in the back seat.

Mom and I decided to take turns sleeping and staying awake. She took her little wind-up travel alarm out of her purse and set it to ring in two hours. I would sleep first, and she would wake me up when it was my turn. It was so cold inside the car that even with all our heavy clothes on and the blankets, we couldn't stop shivering.

I think I fell instantly to sleep, and when she woke me, I checked on my sisters, cocooned under the bedding we shared. Thankfully, they were both sleeping soundly, their breathing regular.

She handed me the alarm clock. I hoped I could stay awake. "I helped myself stay awake by trying to remember everything I could about when I was a little girl," she said. "And, I prayed more. It helped me concentrate and kept me from worrying so much."

"Okay, I'll try to keep busy thinking about stuff," I promised. "I'll wake you when the alarm goes off."

"Lynne," she said. "I'm very proud of how brave you are being. You are a lot of comfort and help. And, I really liked your prayer. I love you, too."

I smiled and sat up straighter in my seat, preparing to take my turn at keeping watch over my family.

We traded off every two hours for what seemed like an

eternity. It was nearly six o'clock when she woke me for the third time. "Is everyone okay?" she asked me. I checked my sisters and they were alive, breathing, but as I watched, each of them shivered violently in their sleep. I shuddered with the cold, too, and tried to wipe my sleepiness away.

"Are you and Jodie okay?" I asked.

"Yes, I think so," she said. "I am a little worried about her. I tried to move her a while ago, and she didn't respond. Maybe she's just very sound asleep, but I am concerned. It is so awfully cold." Her voice was flat.

We were both silent, probably each wondering if any of us would live through this. I was almost too tired to care anymore.

"Get some sleep, Mom," I said. "I'll wake you again at eight."

"It won't be light yet," she said, "but maybe someone will be on the road by then."

She shifted Jodie off from her lap so they could lie down next to each other, and I soon heard her breathing pattern change and knew she was asleep.

To keep awake, I tried to think about school. I pictured where everyone sat in each class, recalling names and faces. I tried to remember the questions on my last science quiz just before the break. I went through the presidents of the United States, starting with George Washington. And I thought about my boyfriend. I tried to picture every pimple and blackhead, the sharpness of his blue eyes, his laughs—both of them—the one he used when we were alone and he was being himself, and the one he used with his friends when he wanted to be noticed.

I pictured our neighborhood and mentally went down one side of the street and back up the other, thinking of every family by name—the parents, the kids, all the various dogs and cats and other pets. I thought about the weird guy and his girlfriend who lived in the little house near the end of the block, the one with pet boa constrictors. I hated walking by his house because he was creepy and made me nervous. Not because of his snakes but the way he looked at me sometimes, like I didn't have all my clothes on and he could see inside.

I remembered the first time I met Ted. Shortly after we'd moved into the neighborhood, some of my friends took me to meet him. His girlfriend was there that time, and he wasn't acting strange that day. My friends had told me about his snakes, but I wasn't prepared to see the living room filled with two gigantic cages and the huge thing coiled up in a corner of each.

"You're in luck," he told us. "It's feeding time." Then he took us out to the filthy back porch to a cage filled with rats. I'd tried to not let on how disgusting I thought they looked, staring up at us with little whiskered faces.

He reached his hand and grabbed a big gray one by its tail. It squealed and tried to climb his arm, but he had a good hold on it, and took it to one of the cages in the living room. I thought the snake was sleeping, but suddenly it began to unwrap itself from the corner and slithered over to the front of the cage. Ted opened the door in the top of the cage and dropped the rat in. It tried to run away from the danger, but the snake had it in just a flash. I watched, horrified but unable to look away, as the snake opened its mouth and began swallowing the rat. It wriggled a few times and then finally stopped. It made a huge bulge in the snake's neck as it slowly slid down its throat.

Remembering the scene now, I again felt the horror of it. I couldn't get the picture out of my mind and it was like I was there again, wanting to run, but too embarrassed to let my friends know how sick it made me feel.

The hair on my neck stood up, just like it had that day, and my hands felt clammy, even inside my mittens.

Without thinking, I leaned back against the car door, as if I was trying to get away from the awful memory.

At that moment, something beat on the door of the car right next to my ear, and suddenly it opened. I screamed.

A black ski mask with only two dark eyes showing was suddenly in my face. Then a giant gloved hand was touching me. Maybe I'd actually dozed off and was dreaming, because for a second I felt like I was the rat, about to be eaten by a huge snake. I screamed again; I just couldn't stop myself. Terrie and Darlene both stirred, but they didn't jump up, like I would have expected for all the noise I was making. They slowly looked around, trying to shake off their deep sleep.

"Where are we?" Terrie asked, like she'd somehow forgotten what had happened.

Darlene grumbled about being so rudely disturbed and she tried to snuggle deeper in the bedding.

In the front seat Mom was wide-awake now, struggling to free herself from Jodie's weight. Jodie whimpered a little, so I knew she was still alive. Mom twisted around to face the big black thing with its head in our car. It had by now pushed past me and it was leaning further into the car.

"Are you okay, ma'am?" a man's voice asked. It felt like his full weight was on me, but I was still too scared to try to move.

Mom didn't answer and when I looked at her to see why, I saw a strange mix of looks crossing her face. Her mouth opened and shut three or four times but no sound came out. She looked disoriented at first, then startled, then scared, then relieved, then like she was about to cry.

Before she could get her bearings and answer him, he backed out of the car and shouted to someone outside. "They're alive. Come give me a hand."

The man grabbed my arm. I felt really strange, like I was in a dream—not really here—more like the real me was home in bed sleeping, having a nightmare. But I wasn't scared anymore.

"Let me help you out of the car," he said. I couldn't seem to move. He pulled on my arm again, and then I felt him put it around my shoulders and his other arm push under my legs. He struggled to lift me out of the car. He helped me stand up and then another man was there. They both put arms around me and helped me walk. They were both very strong and smelled warm, like coffee.

They guided me, step-by-step, to a big car waiting on the road. Steam from the exhaust rose like a cloud into the air and when I saw the emblem on the side, I realized the men were Mounties. "Here, get in and get warmed up," one of them said as he held open the back door.

"My sisters and Mom...," was all I could say.

"Don't worry. We're getting them, too," he said,

patting my arm. He sounded very nice. "You just rest now. We'll be right back."

I was shivering so hard I felt like I might break apart, but now that I could feel the warmth of the car on my cheeks, I knew we would all be okay.

The door opened again, and one of the Mounties lifted Darlene in. She seemed to be more awake now, and not forgetting her manners, like I had, she said, "Thank you, Mr. Policeman."

He smiled at her and patted her cheek. "Snuggle up with your sister there and get warm." Then he was gone again.

It seemed like a long time had gone by, and they hadn't come back. I sat forward so I could look out the window. I was worried that something was wrong with Mom or Jodie.

Finally, I saw some figures moving, coming like ghosts out of the white. A few minutes later the door opened for a third time. Both Mounties were there; one helped Terrie into the back seat with Darlene and me. The other was holding Mom's arm and carrying Jodie. Mom walked like a robot, stiffly, like her knees weren't working. She dropped onto the front seat, and when she got settled, he handed her my littlest sister so Jodie could sit on her lap.

I heard an engine and saw flashing lights moving towards us along the road.

"The tow truck is here," one man said. "I'll stay here and help pull the car out of the ditch. We'll meet you at the lodge later."

"Right-o," said the other man. He walked around the

car and got in the driver's seat. "Here we go, ladies," he said. "Let's get you to some hot food and a nice warm bed." He had a very nice voice.

I was comforted by the sounds of Mom's voice as she and the Mountie talked to each other. She answered his questions. Then she asked one of her own. "How did you know to come looking for us?" I was surprised that I hadn't even thought to wonder, but now I was curious to know his answer.

"The owner of that lodge back down the road checks in with the border station at Tok Junction every morning. The border guard made the comment to him that yesterday's traffic had really been low—only two vehicles all day. The guy at the lodge said there were three—a black pickup early in the day, a red Suburban just after noon, and a white car late in the afternoon. Only the pickup and Suburban had checked through at the border. So they called everyone else who lives along the way, and when it seemed that no one had seen you, they called us and we came looking."

"I'm so glad," Mom said. I looked at her, because the choked sound of her voice told me she was trying hard not to cry. "I was so worried...." She looked over her shoulder toward the back seat. Then she finished her sentence in a whisper, "So afraid we would all die. My poor little girls." Tears were spilling down her cheeks now, and she wiped at her eyes.

The Mountie reached across the seat and squeezed her hand. "There are tissues in the glove box," he said, smiling. "Everything is going to be all right."

The warmth of the car made me feel drowsy. And, now that I knew we were saved, I allowed myself to relax and sleep.

When we got to the lodge, there was a hot meal waiting for us. The hot soup and sandwiches tasted good, but we ate almost without notice, because we were still cold and tired. Then we were helped upstairs and into a big room with two king-sized beds. Mom filled the bathtub with warm water and put Darlene and Jodie into it, scrubbing them down. She dried them off, helped them back into some of their clothes and tucked them into one of the beds. Then Terrie had a turn, and I went next. We snuggled together in the other bed. I was sound asleep by the time Mom had taken her bath and had crawled into bed with the little girls.

We'd slept ten hours before Mom woke us up. She told us Dad was on his way; she'd called to tell him of our adventure (she called it that now, saying that, since it had turned out okay, it was no longer a misadventure), and he wanted to come help us get home safely. We girls could take turns riding in the pickup with him, as he followed Mom in the car.

The tow truck had pulled the car into a warm, enclosed garage, and it had taken hours for the snow that was packed into the engine to melt.

It was night again when Dad finally got there. After supper we sat around the blazing fireplace telling him the story—each our own version. I snuggled into one of the lounge chairs and looked at the faces of my family. Everyone was smiling, and my sisters were even being nice to each other. I knew that what we'd just been through would change us—make us appreciate our lives more.

I closed my eyes and silently thanked God for answering our prayers.

Homecoming

Jo Massey

Betty's hand shook as she struggled to fit the key into the lock of the imposing front door. The cab driver sped away, angrily laying rubber in the circular drive. From her forty some years in the restaurant business, she was well aware how much people in service industries rely on tips, and she understood that he naturally expected a generous tip from someone residing in this posh San Francisco neighborhood. How could he know that she'd barely had enough for the fare to the bank downtown and back? He couldn't possibly know that this was her son's home and she was being held prisoner here. She wasn't really being held hostage, of course, but it felt more like a prison every day.

Nicholas and his family were gone for a week's trip to their new condo in Hawaii, otherwise Betty would never have dared do what she just did. Maybe I'd have been better off if I hadn't, she thought. If I hadn't insisted on finding out the truth I wouldn't have this horrible knot in my throat or pain in my gut.

She could imagine what Gladys, her best friend back in Alaska, might say—"Ignorance is bliss." Gladys' philosophy was what you didn't know couldn't hurt you. For example, it was common knowledge that Gladys' scoundrel husband chased every skirt in the state. But because she, herself, had no real evidence of the fact, she continued to be obliviously happy. Well, that might be okay for Gladys, Betty thought, but that's not the way I'm made up. I need to know where I stand.

The massive door finally gave way, and Betty stepped into the manufactured coolness of the air-conditioned house. She shivered. Such cold. It chilled her more than any of the more than four decades of Alaskan winters she'd lived through!

She absently stepped across the day's mail strewn in a heap beneath the mail slot, not bothering to pick it up. The first morning after Betty had arrived, she'd been amused when the slot in the huge front door flipped open and mail poured through, landing with a hard slap on the marble tiled entryway. She'd stooped to pick it up, and as she did, Nicholas' wife snatched it roughly from her hands, glared at her, and said, "I always sort the mail. Please, just leave it there and I'll handle it."

It had been less than six months since she'd been dragged away from her Alaskan home, and in that length of time Betty felt her life had been turned upside down and left in a shambles. Her ulcer hurt. Her head ached. She hated the damnable impersonal cold of the air conditioning and the formal living room in which she now stood.

Her daughter-in-law made sure this room remained as

uninviting and distant as she was herself. Fragile-looking Japanese porcelain figurines were positioned with precision on expensive, highly polished cherrywood tables that flanked white damask sofas and chairs, cold and uninviting to any ordinary person. Huge modern art paintings in muted tones— bland and boring except for one or two splashes of green, purple, or burgundy smeared across one side—were placed in mathematical exactness on otherwise bare white walls.

The only real color in this austere room, and the only part of it that Betty liked, was the thick, plush carpet, softer than a lot of the beds Betty had slept on. And she rather liked the color, a soft milky green. It reminded her of the Russian River in late spring when the ice had gone off. Fishing that river was one of her passions. She could keep up with the best of them and always chuckled with pride when the men on the river gazed in admiration and amazement as she marched past them—sometimes standing almost shoulder to shoulder along the banks—dragging along her string.

But fishing was not on her mind now as she passed through to the kitchen and began searching for something to relieve the burning in her stomach. It seemed odd to her that she was still so unfamiliar with this kitchen. Most of her life had been spent in kitchens. Yet she was a stranger to this one—had been ever since that first attempt to prepare a meal for her son's family had failed so miserably. "I don't eat red meat," her daughter-in-law had sniffed, disdainfully staring at the platter holding a perfectly prepared beef roast, as if she were being served dog food. "You should know it's fattening," she said, looking pointedly at Betty's size twenty-two figure. "Especially this gravy."

The teenager, Nicholas' stepson, sitting at the opposite end of the table from his mother, stared with disgust at the bowl of steaming potatoes and vegetables. "Yuk, carrots. What is this other stuff? I hate vegetables," he said. Both of them had walked away without either eating a bite, leaving her alone at the table. Perplexed and disappointed, she'd asked Nicholas about it when he came home late from his law office. He told her they were all into health food and that she didn't need to bother cooking for them. They all preferred to eat out or fix their own meals whenever they felt hungry. She audibly sighed now, somehow sensing that she'd find nothing medicinal on these scantily filled shelves.

The door at the far end of the spacious kitchen led to the part of the house that had apparently been designed as servant's quarters and to where she spent her long lonely days. But, instead of going there now, she decided to search further for something to comfort her tormented stomach, knowing Nicholas must have antacid somewhere. She'd occasionally witnessed him gulping big swigs from a bottle he carried in his briefcase. She returned to the living room, then down the long hallway past a number of smaller bedrooms to the double doors leading into the master suite. She felt a pang of guilt before turning the knob and stepping inside. The woman sharing this room with her son had never invited Betty into its confines, acting almost as if it were a shrine.

Betty stopped just inside the door, allowing her eyes to adjust to the semi-darkness. She was surprised at the sensual appointments of the room, so different from the rest of the house. Heavy brocade drapes cascaded from ornate rods, covering floor to ceiling in a sultry shade of French pink. The California king-sized bed was covered in lavish satin of the same pink and smothered with black satin bolsters and pillows. Filmy strips of pink gauze cascaded from ceiling to floor, draping around elaborately carved posts. Shiny black-lacquered chests and dressers, interspersed with numerous mirrors in gold-gilt frames, filled the other walls. The room smelled of lavender and furniture polish.

For a fleeting moment she imagined her son's wife sprawled languidly across the sumptuous bed in one of those French maid costumes from Frederick's of Hollywood, vampishly luring Nick to some unspeakable pleasures. But she shook her head. Impossible, she thought, forcing the image from her mind. She couldn't imagine anything warm or loving about this woman who never addressed her familiarly, not even using her first name, insisting on calling her Mrs. Russell.

She opened the door to their private bath. It was all back to business there—each item in its own predictable place. The antacid was where one might expect it to be, as were the bath towels and toilet tissue. She took the bottle and quickly passed out of the strange bedroom and to her own room at the back of the house.

She swallowed some antacid, closed the blinds, and flopped down on the bed with her shoes still on. She lay flat on her back, rigid and still, staring through the dimmed light at the one blemish on the ceiling, a small watermark the painters had missed. In her mind she ran back through the revelation she'd been given this morning—the revelation that was going to change her life again. It all seemed so sudden.

"Your account has a negative figure," the bank teller had told her when she attempted to draw out a small amount of cash. "You need to deposit at least $537 to bring it to a zero balance. We've sent you several notices telling you that checks were being returned. Surely you've gotten them."

Betty had not received any notices. Her daughter-in-law had undoubtedly destroyed them without giving them to her. And when she insisted that there had to be a serious mistake, that she should, indeed, have more than $80,000 in her account, the bank manager was called in. She waited nervously in his office, seated before his enormous desk— empty except for a telephone and two gold pens sticking from an elaborate holder—while he helped the teller research her account. She watched them through the glass wall separating his room from the main lobby, their heads together pouring over computer printouts. Finally, the man shrugged, shook his head, and slowly walked back to her waiting in his office.

"I'm sorry, Mrs. Russell," he said. "The money was removed from this account over a month ago by the co-signer, Nicholas Russell. He is your husband, I presume?"

"He's my son," she replied. "I didn't know. I'm sorry to have troubled you." She tried to hide her panic, willing her voice to remain calm and steady. But her hands shook as she hailed the waiting taxi. All the money from the sale of her cafe—gone. Her entire life's savings—missing. What had Nicholas done with it, she wondered. The recently acquired condo in Hawaii? His wife's new Porsche safely parked and locked in the oversized garage? College tuition at Princeton for Nicholas' spoiled stepson? She dared not think about it.

In the dim light of her room she closed her eyes and

thought of Alaska. She missed her home and friends more than she would have believed possible. She replayed yet again those conversations with Nicholas. He'd caught her in a rare moment of weakness when he came to visit her in the hospital after her heart attack.

"Mother, you shouldn't be working so hard. Sell the cafe. Come to California and live with us," he persisted. "Now that you're getting old you should be closer to family instead of living way up here where there's no one to take care of you."

She never thought much about her age, but on that day she did feel old, sick, and tired. But even in that weakened condition she'd disagreed with him. "I have a world of friends here who care for me. They are my family. This has been my home for over forty years. I wouldn't dream of leaving."

"But most of those years you had Dad. Now that he's gone there's absolutely no reason you should stay here any longer."

That same day, even as she lay in the hospital recovering, Nicholas posted a "FOR SALE" sign in the window of the cafe and put an ad in the local newspaper. The business sold within the week and Nicholas arranged for his law firm to work with the town attorney to close the deal in record time.

When she'd arrived in San Francisco—a check for the proceeds from the sale safely tucked inside her purse—Nicholas had whisked her directly to the big bank downtown, near his office. "We want a joint account," he told the clerk. When Betty looked at him, bewildered, he explained, "This is so that if anything happens to you, I can take care of your obligations without needing to wait for special legal permission. It's for your own protection."

Remembering that now, she suddenly said, "Bullshit!" speaking out loud to the water spot on the ceiling as if it were Nicholas' own face there. "It was so you could take care of my money. Period." She swung her legs off the bed and sat up. "I'm not going to take this lying down."

In the kitchen, way in the back of the freezer, she found a package of hamburger. She set the microwave to defrost and tossed the meat in to thaw. In the pantry she found a big potato and a purple onion. A big juicy hamburger with a thick slab of onion and homemade French fries would help her think, she was certain. As the meat thawed, she started a pan of oil heating, pared the potato and cut it into long, slender slices.

While her meal cooked, Betty went deliberately to the pile of mail scattered on the living room floor and sorted through it—a glamour magazine, utility bills, a hand engraved invitation to some social function or other, the usual assortment of junk mail filled with advertisements, an official looking notice from the bank, addressed to her, undoubtedly another returned check notice. She was about to toss the pile back onto the floor when she spied familiar handwriting on a blue envelope. It was addressed to her.

She took her letter and returning to the kitchen, began reading.

Dear Betty,

It seems like you've been gone forever. Things just aren't the same around here without you. The men are crankier than ever, especially now that they have something new to grumble about—namely the food being served at Angelino's Ristorante. (Darned pretentious name, if you ask any of us) That Italian bunch that bought your place are running it downhill fast. They don't open up until ten in the morning, so you're just out of luck if you want breakfast. Then, when you finally get inside, the coffee is like something out of a bad dream, so weak you could read the newspaper through it. Food's horrible, too. About the only decent thing on their menu is spaghetti and meatballs. All that stuff with fancy sauces and such are fine for an anniversary dinner or something, but hardly what it takes to keep working stiffs fed right.

I hear tell business is so bad they're about to lose it back to the bank. In fact, Sylvia was by to see me just yesterday and said she hears they're looking for a manager. Sure as hell wish you were here to show them how to run the place!

Betty set the letter aside while she dipped golden fries out of the oil and made her sandwich—hamburger, catsup, pickles, tomato, onion—all in all a totally satisfying, "unhealthy" lunch. She resumed reading where she'd left off.

Most of the rest of the letter was filled with news and gossip of the townsfolk and she smiled or frowned as was appropriate. Towards the end of the letter she read:

Well, if you ever get sick of the big city and want to come home, just call. All your friends here miss you and wish you'd come back. What we need more than anything right now is Betty's Cafe, where a guy can get a decent meal and cup of coffee while swapping lies. Think about it and write soon.

Lovingly, your friend and neighbor,

Gladys

After Betty finished reading, she sat a long time in the cold air-conditioned kitchen staring into space. Still undecided, she walked to the phone, debating whether to pick it up or not. A light on the answering machine was flashing but she ignored it—another of her daughter-in-law's controlling maneuvers. Then, as another act of defiance, she pushed the "play" button and listened in stunned silence to her son's voice. "Mom, are you there? If you're there, pick up." The call must have come while she was at the bank. "Shit," she heard him say under his breath. "Mom, I hope you get this message. I just got a disturbing call from the bank and we're coming home. Our plane leaves in the morning, and we'll be there before noon tomorrow. I'll see you then."

Her decision had just been made easier. She picked up the phone and dialed Alaska.

Next morning Betty stood outside the massive front door of her son's house, a single suitcase beside her, waiting for the cab. Relieved to see a different driver, she said, "The airport, please." Gladys had rallied her community of friends, a collection had been taken up and a ticket to Anchorage was waiting for her. She'd found enough change in a cookie jar for cab fare, and as the driver pulled away from the house and slid into traffic, she didn't even think to look back at the cold, formal house that had held her captive. Instead, she shrank back out of sight as her son's gray Lincoln sped past.

A contingency of her friends met her in Anchorage and the trip home was filled with lighthearted bantering and exchange of news. Gladys had already spoken to the new owners of the cafe and told them Betty was on her way back. They were more than eager to discuss a position for her and, as they had not used her living quarters for anything more than storage, she could move right back in. Her furnishings were also still there, just as she'd left them.

Even with her as the manager, Angelino's continued to flounder. The owners refused to make many of the changes Betty recommended, insisting on doing things their way. She did get them to brew a decent coffee, add a few more basics to the menu, and open earlier in the morning. But even so, she could see it wasn't enough. She was happy to be back home among friends, to have a place to live and a wage that paid her enough to take care of her needs. And she was glad that she didn't have the responsibility of the business while her legal battle with her son was underway.

Nicholas blamed his wife, of course, for the injudicious use of Betty's money. He was contrite and begged her to drop the charges. "If this goes any further, it will ruin me," he pleaded.

She relented, finally, after he and his wife both agreed to sign a promissory note to repay her with full interest once the Hawaiian condo sold. It sold easily, but the proceeds became entangled in their embroiled and ugly divorce settlement that followed, and it took nearly a year before Betty got her check.

After she purchased the business back from the Italians, Betty closed the cafe for a full week in order to ready it for her old customers. An air of festivity seemed to permeate the entire community.

The first snow of the season began to fall on Monday. Huge wet flakes swirled around Mark O'Brien as he stood on a ladder tacking the banner over the doorway—"BETTY'S CAFE Grand Re-Opening," it said.

New menus had just come from the printers, and when the mailman delivered them he stopped to watch Mark work, squinting to keep snow from his eyes. "When's the opening?" he asked.

"Saturday night," Mark answered. "I thought everyone knew."

"Me and the missus will be here. You can count on it," he said. "I wonder what the special's going to be."

"Don't think she's said, but I'm hoping its one of her great pot roasts," Mark replied, climbing down from the ladder.

Jim and Francine Muldoon pulled up and stopped in front. They were both dressed in coveralls and carried buckets of white paint, brushes, and rollers. "We're going to get rid of those depressing green walls!" Francine said. Before the day ended the dining room was a fresh, clean, crisp white. The only traces remaining of the previous owner's presence was a stenciled border painted along the upper edge of the walls—green vines twining around fat clumps of purple grapes. Betty rather liked the framing effect they had, highlighting the room with a touch of color, and she left them unchanged.

The next morning she and Gladys hung cheery yellow lace curtains in all the windows, replacing the heavy, dark green drapes. The green and burgundy table linen left over from the Italian owner were folded away in a box, and new white oilcloth was spread over each table.

"It's beginning to look like home again," Betty remarked.

"It sure is," Gladys said, looking up from where she stood arranging bright plastic daffodils into simple white vases. "Aren't these just the gaudiest things?" she asked, looking at the collection of wine bottles dripping with candle wax. "What do you want me to do with them?" She held one up with her thumb and a finger, as if it were a dog turd.

"Just stick them all in that box. Maybe we'll give them out as door prizes," Betty chuckled. "Or maybe we'll have a garage sale in the spring and sell them back to the Italians."

Sylvia came by the next afternoon with a floor polisher she'd rented while on her regular twice-a-week flight into Anchorage. She and Mark owned three planes now, and with all the hours they each spent flying customers, and making a happy home, they were kept busy. "I'll help you with the floors tonight," she said, "and return this tomorrow when I go back to pick up your grocery order." The linoleum throughout the cafe, including the kitchen, sparkled like new once all the old wax was removed.

Betty began cooking on Friday morning and continued through Saturday. She filled one entire counter with a multitude of pies, making sure to include at least one each of her regular customers' favorites—cherry, blueberry, peach, apple, raisin, lemon meringue, and chocolate. Loaves of homemade bread, three styles of potatoes, a dozen varieties of salads and vegetables, meatloaf, fried chicken, roast pork, a huge smoked ham, and plenty of her famous pot roast—cooked to perfection—were ready when she ceremoniously unlocked the front doors at six p.m. sharp.

The street was lined with vehicles. The entire town seemed to be milling around, standing in groups, talking and laughing, and tramping down the new snow that had been falling in intermittent flurries most of the day. The air was charged with the kind of excitement children exhibit on Christmas Eve—almost as if some celebrity had come to pay a special visit.

"Damned good to have Betty back," one of the fishermen sighed, pinching in the loose fabric on the waist of his trousers. "Look-at here how much weight I lost, yearning for a decent meal!"

"Ah, hell, you been that skinny all your life!" came the retort from one of his companions. "But I agree. This town ain't been the same without our friendly little cafe. I guess after forty years we all kinda took for granted it'd be here forever."

Every table immediately filled. The others who could get inside, stood around the front door, chatting with one another, waiting their turn. Those who couldn't get in continued to mill around outside, engaging in friendly conversations until tables became available, seemingly content to wait.

Betty bustled about the kitchen, supervising Gladys, Sylvia and her other temporary help, making certain that everyone was fed as quickly as possible. Even Timmy, now a pleasant young man, bused the tables. She stopped every now and then by each table to greet her customers and to thank them for coming.

"Now don't be strangers," she said as they paid for their meals. As each group left they complimented her on her cooking and expressed their pleasure that the cafe was back in business.

"We'll be back," everyone promised. And Betty had no reason not to believe them.

It was nearly midnight before Betty had waved goodbye and closed the door behind the last customer, the final dishes were washed and put away, and her help had gone for the night. Betty went to her quarters and took a hot shower. She looked at the face staring back at her from the mirror as she cold-creamed it. She had become accustomed to the lines appearing there, but this time she examined them closer. She was tired and her face showed it. But she smiled, deciding the majority of the lines around her lips and the corners of her eyes were happy ones—the lines of an easy and contented life.

With a satisfied sigh, she pulled on a flannel nightgown, crawled into bed and turned out the light. An image of Judy Garland, and the words "There's no place like home," rang through her mind, lulling her to peaceful sleep.

Printed in the United States
49681LVS00001B/1-39

9 781932 636093